A Christian's Guide *to* Planet Earth

WHY IT MATTERS AND HOW TO CARE FOR IT

BETSY PAINTER

Illustrated by MUTI

ZONDERVAN®

ZONDERVAN

A Christian's Guide to Planet Earth

© 2022 by Karen Elizabeth Painter

Requests for information should be addressed to:
Zondervan, *3900 Sparks Dr. SE, Grand Rapids, Michigan 49546*

ISBN 978-0-3104-5863-0
ISBN 978-0-3104-5856-2 (eBook)
ISBN 978-0-3104-5857-9 (audiobook)

Cover design: Tiffany Forrester
Interior design: Kristen Sasamoto

Printed in China

22 23 24 25 26 DSC 10 9 8 7 6 5 4 3 2 1

To my nieces, Maisy, Winslow, and Rosie.
May you always wonder at God's good creation.
Here's to leaving it in better shape for you.

CONTENTS

FOREWORD

It is a pleasure to write the foreword for Betsy's book, *A Christian's Guide to Planet Earth*. Betsy served as an intern for A Rocha USA while a student at Yale Divinity School. A Rocha USA, where I serve as director, is a nationwide community of Christians working in biodiversity conservation and helping others care for creation, and we were blessed to have her as part of our team, where we experienced firsthand her enthusiasm for God's creation. In this book she offers poignant insights and practical ways to be a responsible Christian in the face of significant ecological challenges.

As we witness the continual destruction of habitat, the over-exploitation of natural resources and species, the pollution of the oceans, or our induced changes to the climate, it all seems intractable and too big to fix. As problems increase, our perceived ability (or inability) to respond meaningfully feels overwhelming and can lead to deep anxieties. An emerging psychological condition called *eco-anxiety* fosters this sense of doom and pending ecological disaster in us. These are not phantom worries we carry around but rational responses to our growing awareness of environmental problems and our direct experiences living as part of God's creation.

At A Rocha USA, people frequently come to us asking, *"What can I do?"* to address these overwhelming problems. Many are Christians who are relieved to find an organization like ours, which is part of a worldwide family of A Rocha organizations that have been carefully attending to creation for nearly forty years, spanning twenty countries. People want to understand which actions they can take to make a positive local and global impact. Knowing where to start can be a challenge.

A Christian's Guide to Planet Earth is an excellent place to start. It offers a wealth of practical information, recommendations, and basic steps for taking action. Betsy provides a helpful overview of why and how to get started that is both scientifically and theologically informed.

One important theme in this book—and one not often explored in this context—is for Christians to sustain hope. Hope, not in the sense of a blind or defiant optimism but out of confidence that all creation is part of God's redemptive purpose. The notion that God's work of salvation extends to *all* creation is challenging for many

Christians. We tend to think primarily of the human family bene-fiting from God's redemption in Christ, but the story is much larger. Certainly, human flourishing is an important aim. Betsy simply encourages us to extend our notions of restoration and flourishing to the nonhuman creation as well.

I think it helps to remind ourselves that this is God's world, and our Creator loves the creation. We are invited into a unique role of service as honored participants in God's redemptive work that extends to the full community of creation and testifies to the hope that God will one day redeem this world and inaugurate the kingdom on earth as it is in heaven.

Betsy provides numerous ways to move toward meaningful action that can make a difference in our lives and on this planet we are privileged to inhabit. My recommendation is to choose one of her ideas or suggestions that captures your imagination and pursue it with enthusiasm.

Mark Purcell, Ed.D.
Executive Director, A Rocha USA

INTRODUCTION

The earth is the LORD's, and everything in it.

PSALM 24:1 NIV

WHAT'S YOUR EARLIEST MEMORY IN NATURE? FOR MANY OF US IT occurred right outside our childhood homes. For me, I was wrist deep in dirt, sitting uphill from a creek lined with oaks and willows. With my mom's garden shovel, I scooped up dirt and molded it into an ant hill and sprinkled grass into the nearby hole to make a bed for grasshoppers. It was an ant and grasshopper duplex.

My childlike faith, fresh as heaven, colored my vision with wonder. Everything I saw and touched was made by God, from the rocks I picked out to the grasshoppers I caught between my fingers.

I felt a giddy delight in my responsibility to care for the critters in my yard as I built them homes.

God has built us a remarkable home, this planet Earth. We can view creation in a variety of ways: as something to be exploited without restraint or as a vague backdrop to the day-to-day activity of our lives, for instance. In this book, though, I hope to offer a different view. It's not a *new* view, rather an ancient way of seeing and interacting with nature that's part of the deep history of the Christian faith.

This book is an invitation to engage with nature and the Creator in a biblical way and wonder at the world through the lens of faith. It's designed to stir your heart to love all of God's creation, to learn to see nature with reverence and kindness. We will reclaim our God-designed connection to the planet and our role in bringing it toward a state of flourishing for God's glory and as a service to people, particularly vulnerable populations, who depend upon it.

> **This book is an invitation to engage with nature and the Creator in a biblical way and wonder at the world through the lens of faith.**

To do this well, we need to equip our minds with the knowledge of how the planet's systems work. We'll explore what the best available science reveals to us about diverse environments, from wetlands to mountains. When I built the ant and grasshopper homes, my motivation was right, but I was wrong about their habitat needs. The ants never noticed their carefully crafted hills, and the grasshoppers (ungratefully) bounded away from their beds. Likewise, without the relevant knowledge, our work can miss the mark. However, when we study and know creation well, we can cultivate and protect it more effectively.

Each of the book's eleven chapters covers a specific aspect of the planetary systems. The book begins by describing each ecosystem or area, its purposes and functions within the planet, and the problems each faces. The next section explores biblical themes and lessons to help awaken our curiosity and appreciation of our Maker's creativity and provision. And finally, I offer practical tips for how we can make a difference. My advice is to choose a few of these tips, whichever ones seem most feasible to accomplish, put them into practice, and then build on them from there.

The intent behind this layout is to help connect our hearts with our actions. It's not meant to overwhelm or burden, but rather to simplify and focus, to help us live more humbly, with great contentment, and with less anxiety attached to cultural consumerism. How we treat the planet, including our purchasing decisions and daily habits, is interwoven with us becoming people who are mindful of each other's needs and demonstrating that through our purchasing decisions and daily habits.

My vocation is an unconventional blend of environmental conservation and Christian ministry, and I entered Yale University for graduate studies to explore more intentionally and deeply the connection I've experienced between the two fields. I've had the privilege of working alongside passionate people in the environmental field who impressed me with their perseverance and disdain for apathy in the face of discouraging news regarding one environmental crisis after another. I wrote this book because I believe my family in the faith has the reason, the hope, and the resources to make a difference.

> We have an opportunity to reflect the gospel message of loving things to life.

We have an opportunity to reflect the gospel message of loving things to life. It's time for the church to step onto the scene amid a struggling creation, roll up our sleeves, and get "wrist deep in dirt" to show the world that we care about our mutual home. Let's look at planet Earth as Christ does: with plans and visions for restoration, healing, and reconciliation with the persistent hope of a Savior who makes all things new.

Join me in this prayer before we begin . . .

Loving Lord of heaven and earth,

Thank You for the detail, care, and love You put into creating planet Earth. Thank You for sharing this living work of art, a vibrant masterpiece, with us and giving us the eyes, ears, and minds to study and delight in all of creation with You. Remind us to receive creation's provisions with gratitude and through gentle means. Help us do our part in our own unique ways to keep the earth thriving for now, and for future generations.

Please give us the Holy Spirit to renew our minds to see the world as You do. Show us where Your earth is broken, lead us to those who are in lack of the planet's practical provisions, and help us work together as a community of faith to heal and restore. We celebrate Your awesome and intricate works and long to engage with all of creation in worship of You. Fill the earth with the knowledge of Your glory and the hope of the promised new heaven and new earth through Your Son, Jesus.

In His wonderful name we pray,
amen.

CHAPTER ONE

FRESH WATER

Our Most Precious and
Scarce Resource

He makes springs pour water into the ravines; it flows between
the mountains. . . . He waters the mountains from his upper
chambers; the land is satisfied by the fruit of his work.

PSALM 104:10, 13 NIV

HAVE YOU EVER STOOD AT THE BOTTOM OF A WATERFALL AS FRESH
water cascades down towers of rock? Mist rises with flickering sunlight casting rainbows around the falls. Have you witnessed the
power of water? This liquid force of nature carved out the Grand
Canyon! Water is breathtaking and awe-inspiring, yet this precious
resource is surprisingly scarce.

What Is Fresh Water?

Fresh water is water that contains less than 1,000 milligrams per
liter of dissolved salts—virtually saltless. This includes streams, rivers, ponds, and lakes, as well as glaciers, ice sheets, and icebergs.
Another vital source of fresh water is found underground, in layers of
porous rock called aquifers. When it rains, water seeps down through
the soil into the aquifer, refilling or recharging it. This groundwater is
drawn up by wells and is especially important for our drinking supply
and for irrigating crops.

One of the most pressing global environmental issues today is lack of access to clean water. This may be perplexing at first, because a quick glance at a globe would suggest that most of the world's surface is covered by the ocean's blues. And you'd be right! Approximately 70 percent of the earth's surface is covered by water. Then why is water shortage a problem? Surprisingly, most of the water on the planet is salt water, meaning it's undrinkable. The oceans and seas all contain salt water, leaving only 3 percent of the earth's water fresh. However, most of this is inaccessible and frozen at the poles, which means only a meager 1 percent is reasonably within reach.

CLEAN WATER CHALLENGES

Even with the limits on our fresh water supply, the real challenge is distributing fresh water to everyone who needs it. More than two billion people lack access to safe drinking water.[1] That's equivalent to double the population of North and South America combined without drinkable water! Inadequate access to water prevents people from meeting their daily needs for hydration, cooking, and sanitation. Can you imagine spending hours of your day walking to get water for your family? That is the reality for many women and children who could be spending that valuable time working or in school.

How bad is the clean water situation? Let's look at a few examples—one overseas and a couple closer to home—to put things in perspective.

Aquifers *and* Wells

ARTESIAN
WELL

FLOWING
ARTESIAN WELL

WATER
TABLE WELL

LAKE

CONFINING
LAYER

UNCONFINED AQUIFER

CLAY

BEDROCK

CONFINED AQUIFER

US Water Contamination: the Cuyahoga River and Flint, Michigan

Not long ago, the United States experienced pollution at alarming levels in its lakes and rivers. In the 1960s, the Cuyahoga River in Ohio was so contaminated from oil leaks and industrial runoff that it burst into flames. This event became a symbol of the American environmental movement and helped initiate the first Earth Day. After the passing of the Clean Water Act in 1972, and extensive work cleaning up and plugging sources of pollution, the river began to recover.

This event became a symbol of the American environmental movement and helped initiate the first Earth Day.

More recently, in 2014, residents in Flint, Michigan, reported that the water in their homes looked dirty, smelled foul, and tasted bad. At the time, the population was predominantly African American, and 45 percent of Flint residents were living below the poverty line.[2] Even after citizens brought the water problem to the attention of officials, nothing was done until the case made it to the federal court in 2016. By that time, thousands of children had been given

←

Humans rely on aquifers for drinking water. These bodies allow water to move up through the saturated rock and sediment, providing the majority of our groundwater. These water-bearing stratums release the water in appreciable amounts, which make up about 37 percent of our drinking water—noting that wells can be drilled into aquifers, for easier potable water access.

lead-contaminated water for over a year,[3] which is especially upsetting since lead is detrimental to a child's growth and development.

A Look at India's Water Challenge

India's freshwater situation is a challenging puzzle to solve. The country's water supply is tied to its wildly oscillating weather, releasing not enough and then too much water, depending on the season. Heat shocks and absent rains cause dry spells, while annual monsoons bring extreme rainfall and damaging floods. If the monsoons arrive late and last for a shorter period, cities become vulnerable to their reservoirs drying up. In some cases the water supply reaches zero. This happened in 2019, in Chennai, India, when the four main reservoirs to the city ran dry, causing a severe water crisis. At the time, twenty-one other Indian cities were also threatened with a dwindling water supply.[4]

In northern India, the Ganges River runs from the Himalayas to the Bay of Bengal. It holds enough water to meet the needs of four hundred million people[5] (more than the population of the United States!), but it's notoriously polluted. Trash, toxic waste, and raw sewage surge into the river from numerous sources, contaminating its supply and causing deadly diseases.

What makes India's water challenges even greater is the dense population and the number of residents living in poverty. Whether the challenges come from erratic climates or deficient infrastructure, our brothers and sisters living in second- and third-world countries are often hit the hardest.

OUR RESPONSIBILITY

Failure to clean up our bodies of water and uphold solutions that protect our water systems can lead to rivers combusting, human illness and death, and food contamination. If we aren't wise with our water consumption and conservation, especially in regions prone to drought, our water tables can shrink to concerning levels.

Prioritizing clean drinking water for everyone is a godly way to care for people.

Water justice in the US involves addressing water issues and protecting clean water sources with the same care and urgency for every community, regardless of race or economic status. Prioritizing clean drinking water for everyone is a godly way to care for people. And we must consider those outside the US—countries and cities with the poorest water quality and least-accessible supply—as we think about who our neighbors are and understand their needs.

A BIBLICAL PERSPECTIVE

When we see a community in need of fresh water, we have an opportunity to reflect God's character. In the book of Matthew, Jesus said that when we offer a cup of water to someone in need, it's as if we were giving the Messiah Himself a drink (10:42). Jesus is very serious about physical provision for His people, and we should be too. God invites you and me to participate in providing fresh water for one another, and when we do, we can be confident that we are becoming more like Christ.

Water Connects Us

As we learn in Genesis 1:2, while creation was still empty and formless, God's Spirit was "hovering over the face of the waters." God had a plan for water to sustain all life on earth. Amazingly, every water molecule God created in the beginning is still a part of the water cycle today! Around the planet, water evaporates, condenses into clouds, then precipitates back to the earth as rain or snow. This natural circulation of water connects the seas and rivers with the forests, grasslands, wetlands, and deserts. It also connects them to you and me. Water is the foundational force that binds each ecosystem to another. Without it, life would fail. When we pollute or contaminate our water, we interfere with the systems God set in place to give and support life.

Water Sustains Us

Humans are intentionally and intricately connected to creation through water. Our bodies contain around 60 percent water, and our brain cells are about 85 percent water. We literally can't think without it! We can't survive more than several days without drinking it. It's how we naturally cool our bodies through sweat and how we express emotion through tears. God *designed* us to need water. Do you ever think about your dependence on water and the natural world? It's pretty incredible to think God created our bodies with water, to continually need water, and to access water through His creation.

Scripture shows us that it matters to God that people have clean water to drink. Through Moses in the book of Exodus, God caused water to gush forth from a rock in the wilderness, without which His people would have surely died. God provided for Jacob to buy a portion of land

> **Scripture shows us that it matters to God that people have clean water to drink.**

and build a well to supply water to his community. In the Old Testament wells were foundational to the survival of a community, especially in a desert setting. These stories show how God knows and meets our needs, bodily as well as spiritually.

Water Renews Us Spiritually

Throughout the Bible, God uses water metaphorically to demonstrate spiritual renewal. Just as God designed our physical bodies to rely on water, our spirits cannot thrive without the transformative presence of God. Perhaps the most notable example of this in a Christian's life is the sacrament of baptism, which signifies the cleansing and spiritual rebirth of our souls. Jesus also used water to wash the disciples' feet. Peter learned he had to let Jesus wash his spirit in order to share in the life of holiness with God the Father. In all these examples God chose water, with its cleansing abilities, to physically demonstrate spiritual change. If God chose to work

God offers us peace in the presence of water.

through and with water, what does that say about this significant substance?

God offers us peace in the presence of water. Psalm 23:2–3 says, "He leads me beside still waters. He restores my soul."

When we take time to sit by a stream and pray, the peace of God settles over us and stills our anxieties to match the tranquil waters. We're restored by enjoying creation and resting in God's presence. The beauty of glistening, rhythmic waters in nature is a gift from our Creator. Someday we'll enjoy life in a perfectly renewed place, but until then, as Christians, we have a responsibility to respect and protect earth.

When we consider what a gift water is—a life-giving, cleansing, satisfying, restorative gift—we see how important it is for us to be good stewards of our water sources and supplies; to do our part in meeting the physical water needs of everyone; and to work for clean, accessible water, especially to marginalized populations.

Conserve Water and Create Lifestyle Habits

Commit to these water-saving tasks in your daily life as a way to practice thoughtful care for water resources in your area. Be mindful every time you use water.

AVOID FAUCET FOULS.

- ▸ Turn off your faucet while it's not in use. Running water while brushing your teeth? That's a faucet foul. Mindfully turn it off.
- ▸ Use a fully loaded dishwasher instead of hand-washing dishes in the sink. Or if hand-washing, use a tub or fill the sink with soapy water, then rinse all at once after washing.

TRY WATERWAY-FRIENDLY CLOTHES WASHING.

- ▸ Piles of clothes to wash and fold can test the best of us. Avoid excessive washing. Hang up your clothes after use to air them out; wash them only when your eyes (or nose) confirm they're dirty.
- ▸ Run the washing machine with a full load. Use the cold setting to save energy.
- ▸ Choose "green" (eco-friendly) laundry detergents (check to make sure they're phosphate-free). Or find a laundry detergent recipe online and concoct your own homemade detergent from simple grocery-store ingredients.
- ▸ Purchase a microfiber filter, like the Guppyfriend laundry bag or the Cora Ball, to catch the textile debris that leaches off clothes and ends up in our wastewater and environment.
- ▸ If purchasing a new washing machine, look for eco-friendly options like EnergyStar, which saves water and electricity.

- Limit your time in the shower to three to eight minutes, or as brief as possible. Pick a couple of songs and challenge yourself to finish showering before they're over (singing along is encouraged).

- Install a low-flow showerhead to save around 60 percent of water usage every month. Look for the WaterSense label. Fix broken toilets and consider water-saving models.

- Test your toilet for leaks. Remove the toilet tank lid, add ten drops of food coloring into the tank, replace the lid (don't flush), wait fifteen minutes, and then check the toilet bowl. If the water is colored, you have a leak and need to have it fixed.

Engage with Your Local Water Sources

Water issues are global, but it's helpful to think locally.

EXPLORE LOCAL RIVERS, LAKES, AND STREAMS.

- The writer of Genesis mentioned the rivers flowing out of Eden by name—Tigris, Euphrates, Pishon, and Gihon. Do you know the names of the bodies of water in your area?

- Contact your local utility company to ask where your water is sourced from. Visit and pray by these vital freshwater ecosystems.

LITTER CLEANUPS, PLUS OUTDOOR SPORTS.

- Organize a litter cleanup by foot, kayak, or canoe with your church or neighborhood. Bring trash bags and map out a route.

- If walking, prioritize trash thrown in street gutters, which ends up in our rivers and lakes. If boating, look for litter on the banks and floating in the water.

- Check online to see if any organized "Blueway Cleanups" are happening in your area.

Incorporate Water-Friendly Lawn-Care Practices

What you do right outside your house and in your neighborhood makes a difference. By appreciating your local water supply and using only as much water as you need, you can be mindful of those who don't readily have access to clean water.

EXPERIMENT WITH XERISCAPING.

- Lawns covered in one type of grass are inefficient water guzzlers. Xeriscaping is a landscaping method designed to limit or eliminate the need for watering.
- Replace grass with a combination of soil, rocks, mulch, and native plants like shrubs, cacti, succulents, wildflowers, and trees.
- Some drought-resistant plants include cacti, agave, juniper, and lavender. Plant herbs and spices like thyme, sage, and oregano.[6]
- Make sure to choose native plants. Once established, they do well with not much more than normal rainfall.

Support Water-Focused Nonprofits

Consider supporting one of these groups to help your neighbors around the world.

- **Living Water International** is a faith-based organization that has completed more than 21,000 clean-water projects globally.
- **World Hope International** brings clean water, energy, and economic empowerment to vulnerable populations.
- **Swechha** is a youth-led organization in India that cleans up rivers and uses the litter to make or "upcycle" merchandise.

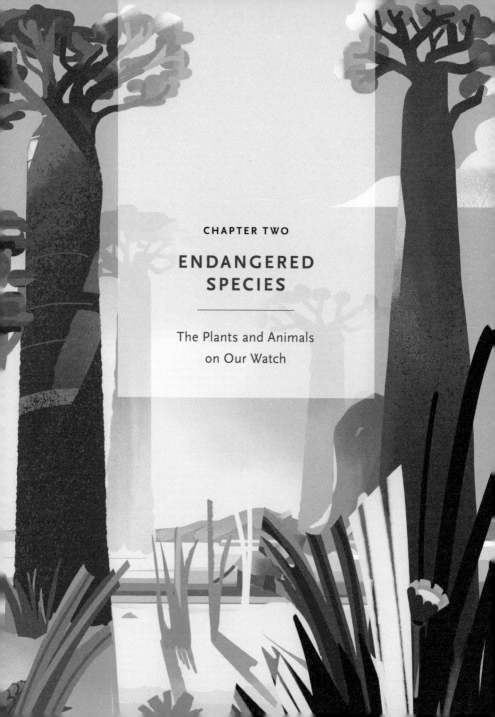

CHAPTER TWO

ENDANGERED SPECIES

The Plants and Animals
on Our Watch

Praise the LORD, all his works everywhere in his dominion.

PSALM 103:22 (NIV)

DID YOU KNOW WE'VE IDENTIFIED AROUND 1.6 MILLION DIFFERENT living creatures on the planet? But incredibly, it's estimated that there may be as many as 8.7 million or more in existence.[1] Basically, for every living creature we know about, there may be five or six more we *don't* know about!

Unfortunately, many of these species go extinct every day, often without our observation. The causes can be natural, but the current extinction rate for species has reached unprecedented levels—tens

What Are Endangered Species?

Endangered species are plants and animals whose group numbers are dwindling as they move closer and closer to extinction. The risk of extinction is ranked by three levels: vulnerable, endangered, or critically endangered (the threat increasing with each level). A plant or animal can become extinct in one region, yet still exist in other areas, or they can disappear entirely from the globe.

to hundreds of times higher than the usual rate.[2] Scientists refer to this event as the Sixth Mass Extinction, and it's human caused and accelerating.[3] Can you imagine a world where no tigers roam or blue whales swim? We grew up sharing the earth with many creatures that are now on the brink of existing only in memory. We've become accustomed to having them around, but we need to be intentional to make sure there's space for them to stay.

BIODIVERSITY AT PLAY

Once an endangered species is gone, it leaves an empty hole in its habitat, the home it shares with other living things. It can no longer perform the special job it once filled to keep the ecosystem balanced. Sometimes another creature in the habitat can step in and perform the needed position, like a backup player waiting on the bench to enter a sports match. But as we lose more species, the pool of available replacements diminishes. This is why an abundant variety of species—also known as biodiversity—is tremendously important to the planet. The natural world thrives when it's bountifully biodiverse. As we lose each species, the biodiversity of its habitat declines and the stability breaks down. The benefits that ecosystem provides—like clean air, water, food, medicines, and recreation—are then at stake.

> Can you imagine a world where no tigers roam or blue whales swim?

The **Endangerment** of *Tigers*

SCIENTIFIC NAME: *Panthera tigris*

The Sunda tiger once thrived across the Sunda islands of Indonesia, but now less than 400 remain on Sumatra, with the Bava and Javi tigers now extinct.

Tiger hunting began in the 1600s during big game safaris.

97% of the world's wild tiger population has been lost.

An estimated 3,900 individual tigers remain in the world as of 2021.

Tiger bones are in high demand for products like tiger wine and tiger paste.

Of the original 9 subspecies, 3 have become extinct in the last 80 years.

In Traditional Chinese Medicine (TCM), tiger parts are used for medicinal purposes.

A century ago, more than 100,000 tigers roamed the earth.

The South China tiger is now considered functionally extinct, with zero sightings in the wild for decades.

KEYSTONE SPECIES

When sea otters were overharvested during a boom in the fur trade in the eighteenth and nineteenth centuries, the sea urchins they ate were no longer kept in check. Spiky clusters of urchins took over underwater forests of kelp, destroying the homes of many other animals like seals and octopuses. The otters were a *keystone species*, a species that has a disproportionately large impact on the health of a habitat.[5]

Endangered species projects often focus on the charismatic species, like leopards, elephants, and pandas. This can be a good conservation tactic because most of these megafauna, as they're called, are keystone species—and by protecting them, many other species are saved. But an endangered species can be anything from a bird, mammal, or tree to a fungi, snail, sponge, or insect. No matter its size or appearance, each species plays a purposeful and significant role in the function of its natural home. Every species matters in our

Every species matters in our interconnected ecosystems.

←

Tigers have faced extinction since the 1970s, when their population dropped to fewer than four thousand remaining in the wild. Poaching, fragmentation, and habitat loss have led to their endangerment. Unless wildlife conservationists succeed at protecting both the animals and their habitats, it's estimated that tigers could become extinct in the next twenty years.[4]

interconnected ecosystems, and each requires our attention when it's threatened with extinction, especially when this endangerment happens due to human actions.

CAUSES OF ENDANGERMENT

The greatest threats to endangered species and the associated loss of biodiversity are connected to human activity. These threats include habitat loss, overexploitation, pollution, invasive species, and climate change.

Habitat Loss

Habitat loss is the leading cause of extinction. When we destroy, shrink, or deplete wildlife habitat for human development, wild animals become crowded in the fragmented land and are forced to interact more with humans (and often suffer). When wildlife and humans are in closer proximity, what's known as *human-wildlife conflict* increases.

As humans continue to move into wildlife territory, we need to create and establish innovative ways of coexisting with the animals.

For example, this conflict occurs between farmers and snow leopards. These big cats with gray-green eyes and full, white fur covered in black rosettes are disappearing in the cliffs and rocks of the Himalayas, with estimates of only 4,500 to 7,500 left on the entire planet.[6] One reason is that their prey—blue sheep, ibex, marmots, pikas, and hares—are also diminishing. As a result, the snow leopards will often attack farmers' livestock for food instead, and the farmers retaliate by killing the snow leopards to protect their livelihoods. As humans continue to move into wildlife territory, we need to create and establish innovative ways of coexisting with the animals, such as using livestock corrals designed to keep big cats out.

Overexploitation

Overexploitation is a major contributor to species endangerment. Fully human-made and human-supported, overexploitation involves harvesting wildlife at a level beyond the ability for a population to rebound, and includes the illicit wildlife trade where plants and animals are trafficked illegally for their fur and other products. Poachers kill tens of thousands of elephants in Africa and Asia every year for their ivory tusks. After the US, China, and other countries banned the ivory trade, demand for tusks steadily decreased, but illegal poaching and ivory trafficking still exist, mostly due to weak law enforcement and corruption within the system.[7]

Elephants aren't the only victims. Poachers kill rhinos for their horns, which are used in traditional Chinese medicines and are believed to have healing powers. However, the horns are made of keratin, the same substance as fingernails. There's no scientific evidence to date that rhino horn can cure what ails the people who use them, but unfortunately, ancient texts and traditional practices keep this going, even against sound arguments.[8]

Diseases

Another issue that arises from the mismanagement of wildlife is the spread of zoonotic diseases (diseases that are transmitted from wildlife to livestock and people). From Ebola to West Nile virus and Lyme disease, illnesses that "jump" from wildlife to humans are increasing. Currently, the theory is that the COVID-19 pandemic originated from either a leak out of a lab or from wildlife, likely bats and possibly pangolins.[9]

> We must do better to preserve all creatures for their survival— and ours.

Pangolins are gentle mammals with scales that protect them like armor when they're frightened and roll up into balls. Their scales are prized for use in traditional medicines, and their meat is considered a luxury in some cultures. For this reason, they're the most illegally trafficked mammal in the world and are threatened with extinction. Within the black market, pangolins are crammed together in unsanitary quarters, creating a prime opportunity for disease to spread. This is one reason pangolins were suspected as intermediate hosts for the COVID-19 virus to transfer to people.[10]

Pandemics and endemics are tragic examples of what can happen when we don't manage wildlife responsibly. When we care for wildlife well, we also help prevent future pandemics and the associated human suffering. We must do better to preserve all creatures for their survival—and ours.

A BIBLICAL PERSPECTIVE

In Genesis 2:19 we read, "Now out of the ground the LORD God had formed every beast of the field and every bird of the heavens and brought them to the man to see what he would call them." Humanity's first task was to observe and name each animal. God could have named them, but He wanted to collaborate with us to share in the innate joy of creation.

God's Creativity on Display

Biodiversity and the countless varieties of life on earth point to the endless creativity of the Maker, who made every living thing through and for Jesus (Colossians 1:16). That's startling! Every plant, worm, chipmunk, and flower—whatever you might see during a daily walk—was made through Jesus. Each one has a godly charm, an essence that points back to Christ.

There's a theological word for this unique design placed in each creature. It's called *haecceity*—the traits and essence of a created thing that are unique to that particular being, its divinely given originality. Every detailed component represents or communicates something specific about God, like how a painting or sculpture says something about the artist, whether explicitly or mysteriously. Romans 1:20 says, "For his invisible attributes, namely, his eternal power and

Each one has a godly charm, an essence that points back to Christ.

divine nature, have been clearly perceived, ever since the creation of the world, in the things that have been made." Each species is a part of the puzzle of God's manifested glory in nature and should be safeguarded and cherished as such.

Our Humble Dominion

Beyond naming plants and animals, God also gave us dominion over every living thing. "Be fruitful and multiply and fill the earth and subdue it, and have dominion over the fish of the sea and over the birds of the heavens and over every living thing that moves on the earth" (Genesis 1:28). We need to understand what dominion means in the passage to rightly understand our relationship to nature.

Dominion involves the authority of ruling, not with worldly power but rather in the example of how Jesus rules as King. We are God's representatives on the earth, and it's our responsibility to exercise leadership as Christ would. Jesus cleansed, healed, and restored everywhere He went. Even though He was God, He humbled himself (Philippians 2:8). He came to serve, not to be served (Matthew 20:28), and we are called to be like Him. We are invited to servant leadership as those who care for God's creation. In this humble spirit we can work to make sure habitats remain biodiverse and stable for future generations, and

> **We are God's representatives on the earth, and it's our responsibility to exercise leadership as Christ would.**

endangered species are protected and not ushered into extinction by preventable actions.

Psalm 145:9 says the Lord's "tender mercies are over all His works" (NKJV). God cares for every living creature He has made. We honor God's creation and extend godly mercy through our conservation actions. God has put the care of these creatures into our hands, a noble and humbling role. It's a sobering responsibility. We have a divine call to protect the creatures and creation.

Engage with Local Endangered Species Conservation

Local species are an irreplaceable part of the biodiversity that makes habitats resilient. Even the more obscure and unseemly (or rather, the less aesthetically blessed) creatures—worms, snails, mussels, rodents, and cockroaches—perform foundational and vital roles in habitats.

COMBAT INVASIVE SPECIES.

Plants and animals that are introduced to an ecosystem from an outside source, often by humans, and harm native plants and animals are called *invasive species*. They disrupt habitats and outcompete and eradicate species that were once thriving there, especially endangered ones.

- ► Clean your hiking and fishing gear, and your boat, kayak, or paddleboard before transferring to a new location. Nobody wants to be the person who inadvertently carries an invasive species to where it establishes and causes harm!

- ► Don't move firewood, which often hosts creatures like the emerald ash borer (a highly disruptive invasive species) and tree-killing insects and diseases. Purchase from local firewood providers.

- ► Volunteer at invasive-species removal efforts, your local park, refuge, or other wildlife area. Tackle and weed out those invasives in your yard, like English ivy on trees.

- ► Don't release your pets, like aquarium fish and plants or other exotic animals, into the wild. Your sweet pet goldfish could grow gigantic and disrupt a lake ecosystem.[11] No joke, this happens!

Stop Illegal Wildlife Trafficking

The Convention on International Trade in Endangered Species of Wild Fauna and Flora (CITES) regulates and bans the international trade in endangered wild animals and plants.

- ▸ Avoid purchasing ivory or anything made with ivory. Even if a seller claims the ivory is an antique, raise your eyebrow to subtly show suspicion and say no thank you.

- ▸ Steer clear of Russian caviar and shark fin soup or pangolin meat. Doesn't sound especially appetizing anyway, to be honest.

- ▸ Avoid jewelry made from tortoiseshell. Be aware of boots, handbags, and other items made from sea turtle skin. Baby turtles are cute; these items are not.

- ▸ The trade in furs from most wild cats, seals, polar bears, and sea otters is illegal. Rock the faux fur instead.

- ▸ Check the labels on traditional medicines. Avoid products that list ingredients from tiger, rhinoceros, leopard, Asiatic black bear, or musk deer.

- ▸ Check to be sure leather products like shoes, wallets, handbags, and watchbands aren't made from protected species (like some snakes, crocodiles, and lizards). Cruelty-free leather alternatives, like those made from mushrooms or recycled rubber, are in!

- ▸ Exotic pet imports are likely prohibited, including primates, wild birds, and reptiles. If purchasing an exotic pet, be diligent to discover its origin.[12]

- ▸ Report illegal wildlife trade activities to the U.S. Fish and Wildlife Service.

Get Involved in Global Endangered Species Conservation

Endangered species are all around the world. We can support conservation projects abroad and be intentional with the products we purchase.

CHAMPION HUMAN-WILDLIFE CONFLICT PROJECTS.

Finding creative solutions to human-wildlife conflict is necessary to help people and wildlife coexist as they continually move into closer proximity.

- ▸ Follow and donate to the Snow Leopard Trust, which is building predator-proof corrals with herders and creating reserves for wild snow leopard prey in India to reduce predation on farmers' livestock.
- ▸ The African Wildlife Foundation in Uganda prevents human-wildlife conflict from elephants accidentally trampling farmers' crops by creating elephant deterrents, like hanging chili peppers on fences. It's simple and brilliant!

SUPPORT RANGERS ON THE FRONTLINES.

- ▸ Help assist and equip the rangers in countries that are home to species—elephants, rhinos, lions, etc.—threatened by poachers. Rangers need protection and gear to protect the animals and parks. These guys are legit heroes.
- ▸ The World Wildlife Fund (WWF) has a "Back a Ranger" project, which helps provide rangers with equipment, training, and resources to prevent wildlife crime.
- ▸ African Parks, a non-governmental organization (NGO) focused on conservation, manages African national parks and has the greatest protective force of any NGO across Africa. Research the organization to learn more about how you can help.

UPHOLD THE ENDANGERED SPECIES ACT.

- ▸ The Endangered Species Act (ESA) of 1973 protects threatened species and their habitats in part by requiring development projects to attain permits when the project may impact an endangered species. The ESA also restricts or outlaws the hunting of an at-risk species.

- ▸ The ESA has an impressive success rate—99 percent of species protected under it have avoided extinction. It's brought back many species from the brink of extinction, including the bald eagle, peregrine falcon, gray wolf, and grizzly bear.

- ▸ At times, certain administrations can try to weaken the ESA through legislation and deregulation. Safeguard the ESA by voicing your support, and contact your state senators and representatives.

- ▸ The Endangered Species Coalition website offers downloadable materials to assist people who meet with decision makers that help inform them about the importance of protecting endangered species.[13]

CHAPTER THREE

MOUNTAINS AND MINERALS

The Peaks and Possessions We Prize

> In his hand are the depths of the earth, and
> the mountain peaks belong to him.
>
> PSALM 95:4 NIV

FROM MOUNTAIN PEAKS SILHOUETTED AGAINST SKIES TO GEMS concealed underground, planet Earth arrests our attention and surprises us. You may not realize it, but you are connected to mountains and minerals every day. Some of our most prized possessions and materials come from the land, but we don't always think about the process of how they get from the earth to our jewelry boxes, cars, and homes.

> In the United States it's estimated that each person uses more than three million pounds of rocks, minerals, and metals in their lifetime.

Rocks and minerals are found in an astonishing amount of objects we benefit from every day. Minerals make up the steel and aluminum used in car, train, plane, and boat manufacturing. They're used to create things like our ceramics, countertops, glass, cutlery, surgical scalpels, electrical wires, concrete, and pencils. We use mineral salt to flavor our food and calcium carbonate for baking bread and cakes. In the United States it's estimated that each person uses more than three million pounds of rocks, minerals, and metals in their lifetime.[1] That's a hefty weight! We can consciously lighten our mineral load by reducing our consumption and buying products made from recycled materials when possible.

THE UPSIDE AND DOWNSIDE OF MINING

We extract minerals from the crust, or the outer layer of the earth, to manufacture all the aforementioned products. Our daily activities are linked to the depths of the earth! The reality is that people interact every day with a product that relies on mining. Mines are

What Are Minerals?

Minerals are inorganic solids made up of specific elements bonded together in orderly and repeated crystal arrangements. They occur naturally in the earth and are the building blocks of rocks. For example, granite rock is a combination of mostly quartz and feldspar minerals. More than four thousand minerals have been discovered on the planet. Some mineral crystals are cut and polished into gems—rubies, emeralds, turquoise, jade, and other precious jewels—but other important minerals form ore deposits containing metals like copper, iron, gold, and silver.

a source of income for many communities and provide jobs down the production and supply chains, but the shadow this gift casts is that many mining practices cause long-term destruction. Blasting techniques, for example, are especially detrimental to the land and for the communities that count on its continued productivity.

Mining sites require strict regulations to prevent worker hazards and severe damage to the environment. Even still, when precautions are overlooked, mines can collapse and cause deadly landslides, and explosions and fires can be fatal for miners. Once the mining operations come to an end, pits need to be filled and the land restored, but these steps are often neglected.

It's unrealistic that we will ever eliminate mining practices, but, as with most environmental activities, there are remedial ways of mining the land that are less harmful in the long run. Lower-impact mining techniques, reuse of mining waste, and rehabilitation of mining sites are a few practices we can support.[2]

Mining Rare Earth Metals

In China, mining rare earth metals for the manufacturing of high-tech products, such as smartphones, wind turbines, and electric vehicles (EV), spiked in the 1990s. The chemicals used to extract these elements from the earth led to soil and water contamination, and upturning the earth scarred the land. After public protests, the Chinese government responded with stricter mining regulations.[3] Many mines were shut down, and local and federal officials led cleanup initiatives that included wastewater treatment facilities and planting vegetation like bamboo and grasses to cover barren areas and stop erosion.[4]

There are often trade-offs when choosing between environmentally conscious products and human needs. EVs and wind turbines are instrumental to a more promising future for us and the environment, but we must work to ensure that the processes behind making them (like mining rare earth metals, in this case) avoid as much planetary harm as possible. Even eco-friendly goods need accountability from beginning production to final use. For example, for the rare earth metals in our electronics, like iPhones, a solution is to recycle them properly so their parts can be reused for future products.

Our daily activities are linked to the depths of the earth!

Mountaintop Removal

Mountaintop removal is another controversial mining activity. It's a relatively new method for harvesting coal—a known environmental pollutant—by blasting mountain peaks and knolls. It not only defaces mountains, but millions of tons of rock, sand, and coal debris from the explosions are discarded in the valleys and end up polluting waterways and the atmosphere. This mining practice has been especially controversial in the central Appalachian Mountains, where communities near the mines suffer from an increase in cardiovascular disease, lung cancer, and birth defects.[5]

Blood Diamonds

What if I told you that another example of irresponsible mining may be traced back to your finger? Literally. Blood diamonds, or conflict diamonds, are gems that are mined and used by rebel movements to fund and fuel violence and war. In Angola, the Democratic Republic of Congo, Liberia, and Sierra Leone, the diamond trade has funded weapon purchases that kept armed opposition groups at large, which led to unspeakable atrocities to civilians and inhumane acts of terror.

In addition to diamonds, the mining of colored gemstones isn't a guaranteed cruelty-free operation either. The upheaval of earth damages ecosystems and can pollute watersheds. Unearthing crystals such as emeralds, rubies, and sapphires can be hazardous to the workers and communities, yet at the same time, mining can be a way for rural families to break out of the cycle of poverty. These communities need resources and training for safer working conditions and environmental practices. Although many countries have laws in place instating a minimum age for workers, the International Labour Organization (ILO) has documented continued cases of

Minerals and gemstones form under various conditions in the earth's crust, with the exception of diamond and peridot, which form much deeper in the earth's mantle where magma is found. Through what's called the *igneous process*, magma rises through volcanic pipes to the crust and cools, crystallizing and forming minerals and a long list of precious gemstones.

The Formation *of* Minerals *and* Gemstones

Weather eroding
the mountain

Slow uplift to the surface

IGNEOUS ROCK

**OPAL
MALACHITE**

Sedimentary
layer

Crystallization
of magma

**RUBY
SAPPHIRE**

Compaction &
cementation

**MAGMA
CHAMBER**

SEDIMENTARY ROCK

Melting

DIAMOND PERIDOTS

Burial, high temperatures,
& pressures

Magma from
crust and mantle
(under all layers)

METAMORPHIC ROCK

child labor in mines and in the gem-cutting and polishing phases.[6] How heartbreaking. It's simply unacceptable.

OUR RESPONSIBILITY

Jewels have inherent beauty, and as we'll see, admiring and acquiring them is not wrong. But we have to ask ourselves: At what cost? We can't afford to overlook where our possessions and materials are coming from, and we can't ignore human suffering when it's part of the process. As consumers, we have a responsibility to move the global mining sector toward more humane and environmentally aware activities, to create safer work opportunities, and to keep the land productive for the communities that depend on it.

So how do we treat the planet now, while we wait for our lasting renewed and unshakable home (Hebrews 12:28)? Are we living in a holy way if we take from the earth out of greed without giving back and restoring it to health for future generations?

A BIBLICAL PERSPECTIVE

How do we reconcile that we benefit unawares from goods and resources from the earth sourced by ungodly means—that we often commit sins of omission? We can acknowledge and grieve our oversight and complicity and receive God's grace through the cross, on which Jesus carried our greed and destructive habits. In Him we can have the foresight and motivation to make changes. The first step is to start recognizing that the way we treat the environment is a part of holy, godly living. God has given us the ability to steward the temporary treasures of earth in ways that reflect His goodness, uphold His natural world, and serve the people who rely on it.

Are we living in a holy way if we take from the earth out of greed without giving back and restoring it to health for future generations?

Minerals and gemstones are resources and provisions for our practical necessities, but we need to be mindful of our unchecked greed. The precious jewels and metals of the earth were patiently wrought under the power and provision of God. Their extraction and use should match His character and ways.

The Mountains and God Protect Us

Many times in Scripture, God's people took refuge in the cliffs and caves of mountains when they were in danger. In Psalm 121, the psalmist looked up to the mountains for help from the Lord.

God Himself is compared to the mountains as our refuge and strong shelter. Psalm 125:2 says, "As the mountains surround Jerusalem, so the LORD surrounds his people both now and forevermore" (NIV). Yet God is greater and more steadfast than the sturdiest mountain range.

In the words of Psalm 46:1–3,

> God is our refuge and strength,
>> an ever-present help in trouble.
> Therefore we will not fear, though the earth
>> give way
>>> and the mountains fall into the heart
>>> of the sea,
> though its waters roar and foam
>> and the mountains quake with their
>> surging. (NIV)

The Minerals Are God's Unique Creation

"Surely there is a mine for silver, and a place for gold that they refine. Iron is taken out of the earth, and copper is smelted from the ore. . . . As for the earth, out of it comes bread, but underneath it is turned up as by fire. Its stones are the place of sapphires, and it has dust of gold" (Job 28:1–2, 5–6).

This concealed geological work over millennia reveals the wonders of the great Alchemist, Christ.

Silver, sapphires, opals, and gold—all the precious metals and gems—were fashioned and formed in the chasms of creation, watched and chaperoned by God. For the one-of-a-kind crystals to grow, each mineral required specific conditions and ingredients: the right mixture of elements, intense pressure, high temperatures, space, and time. Cracks and fissures deep in the ground created these rare settings for the formation of the vast variety of minerals, scattered and hidden around the globe. This concealed geological work over millennia reveals the wonders of the great Alchemist, Christ. John 1:3 says, "Through him all things were made; without him nothing was made that has been made" (NIV). He is the melder of minerals and knows the location of each deposit.

Durable Beauty

Precious gems and metals also teach us something about a durable beauty that outlasts eras and kingdoms, concealed beneath landscapes, and discovered only when purposefully sought out. This offers a stunning metaphor about the kingdom of God. Matthew 13:44 says, "The kingdom of heaven is like treasure hidden in a field, which a man found and covered up. Then in his joy he goes and sells all that he has and buys that field." Consider the treasure in this metaphor. Could it be a collection of rubies or other gems buried and discovered in a field?

The treasures of the kingdom of God are like gemstones in their durability and worth—almost indestructible, lasting centuries. Other resources rust or decay more readily and can be compared to the goods and riches of this world that eventually fade away. But the treasures of the kingdom outshine and outlast (Matthew 6:19–21), enduring forever.

Practice Electronic Waste (E-waste) Solutions

There are innovative ways of acquiring the materials to manufacture new products without having to extract raw materials from the earth. For example, we've piloted "mining" from landfills for valuable metals and materials to insert back into the production process. One of the best, readily available solutions is recycling our electronics!

BUY LESS; PRACTICE MINIMALISM.

- ► We're constantly tempted to buy the newest edition of our devices (phones, laptops, watches, televisions, etc.), even when our current ones work fine. You have the ability to resist this! Learn to be content with and take care of the current items in your possession.

- ► Buy electronics only when your current ones are truly damaged or unusable. Buy refurbished products when possible (which also saves money!).

UPCYCLE.

- ► Upcycling, or creative reuse, finds innovative ways to reuse, share, swap out, and repurpose our goods. Thrift shops and garage sales are a great place to find secondhand household items and appliances.

- ► Join or start community or neighborhood forums where you can give, take, or swap appliances for free. Join local "Buy Nothing" and other similar groups on Facebook.

RECYCLE YOUR ELECTRONICS PROPERLY.

- ► Our electronics can't be recycled along with our other waste because they require a more detailed process of shredding, sorting, and separating out the reusable parts. For every million cell phones recycled, we can recover 35 thousand pounds of copper, 772 pounds of silver, 75 pounds of gold, and 33 pounds of palladium.[7]

▸ Many high-tech products we purchase aren't made with longevity in mind. As long as this remains the case, we need to recycle our electronics responsibly (many contain toxins and don't belong in landfills).

▸ Correctly dispose of your e-waste by taking it to stores like Best Buy and Staples that will recycle them for you. Or check out the websites GreenerGadgets and Call2Recycle.

Use Your Purchasing Power

Make informed purchases to ensure the jewelry that makes you feel extra beautiful also helps beautify the planet and protect people from harm. Help increase the demand for minerals sourced and processed through ethical practices, which will then lead to improved conditions for miners, cutters, and communities around the world.

REWARD ENVIRONMENTALLY RESPONSIBLE COMPANIES.

When it comes to ethically sourced minerals, the supply chain is key. Tracing a mineral from one specific mine all the way to the point of sale can be challenging. A gemstone or precious metal is often mined in one country and then traded, exported, and processed in another. Then it's manufactured into jewelry in plants and workshops and finally sold to retailers. By the time the piece is for sale, it may be very difficult to know its origin.[8] Here are some insights on organizations and companies that can help:

▸ Buy jewelry from companies that have moved forward in sourcing their gems, silver, and gold responsibly. The Responsible Jewelry Council (RJC) is a leading organization in setting ethical standards for the worldwide jewelry and watch industry.

- More than 1,200 companies are members of RJC. You can look up companies online to see which ones have achieved the highest certification standards, including the "chain of custody" standard, which requires documentation for adherence to ethical standards along the supply chain.

- Tiffany & Co. can trace all its newly mined gold back to one mine, and it regularly checks in on the mining activities.

- Pandora is another jewelry company that is setting an example by ensuring a moral supply chain from the bottom up.

- Canada's Fair Trade Jewellery Co. imports gold that is fully traceable from artisanal mines in the Democratic Republic of Congo. A growing number of jewelers are sourcing from artisanal mines certified under the Fairtrade or the Fairmined gold standard. Look for this category of gold when purchasing.[9]

- The Maendeleo Diamond Standards (a step up from the original conflict-free diamond certification, the Kimberley Process) focus on labor conditions, child labor law enforcement, and environmental protection.

- Sustainable, ethical gems can also be purchased through small producers and specialist traders. Check out Nineteen48, Fair Trade Gemstones, Gemstones Brazil, Stuller, and Columbia Gem House.

BUY RECYCLED JEWELRY.

- Jewelry made from recycled material or secondhand jewelry are good sustainable options. Some refineries only source metals that can be melted and reused.

- Small jewelry businesses that support ethical fashion can incorporate a combination of recycled materials, ethically sourced gems, and even lab-grown diamonds. Check out Valley Rose, Ten Thousand Villages, Taylor & Hart, Made Trade, Arlokea, Aid Through Trade, and ABLE.

CONSIDER SYNTHETIC GEMS.

▸ Gems made in labs can be a sustainable, conflict-free option. Make sure to ask synthetic gem retailers about the labor conditions of their gem cutters and workers.

Participate in Activism for Ethical Practices

Take the time to research more about the complex problems of ore mining, mountaintop removal, and conflict gemstones. Find a cause that you care about and consider supporting financially or volunteering your time.

SUPPORT CAMPAIGNS.

▸ Christians for the Mountains works within mountaintop removal issues, with the central Appalachian region as its geographical focus.

▸ Amnesty International and Global Witness put pressure on the diamond industry to improve and efficiently implement the Kimberley Process (a global tracking system to confirm the sources of gems, ensuring they're not from a war zone).

CHAPTER FOUR

AIR AND SKY

Our Breath and View
of the Heavens

> For great is your love, higher than the heavens; your
> faithfulness reaches to the skies. Be exalted, O God,
> above the heavens; let your glory be over all the earth.
>
> PSALM 108:4–5 (NIV)

THE SKY IS SPECTACULAR. IT CONDUCTS ELECTRICITY, AND LIGHT-ning cracks in sporadic webs of white-hot light. Solar flares interact with the earth's magnetic field and atmospheric gases to create the glowing emerald and magenta waves of the auroras. Sunsets and sunrises daily draw people to wonder at creation. They're God's paintings, sky canvases displaying His majesty.

When we look up from earth, every star we see with the naked eye is part of our galaxy. In some remote places the sky is clear enough to see the Milky Way and Andromeda galaxies. When we look down on earth from spacecrafts at night, we see a network of iridescent lights clustered in cities and spread out across towns. We live in an incredible time of technology and space exploration that allows us to see and explore what the

They're God's paintings, sky canvases displaying His majesty.

psalmist called "the heavens." The air and sky above us are expansive and lovely, as we know from stargazing, storm-watching, sunrises, and sunsets—and they are worth considering and protecting.

THE HARMFUL EFFECTS OF POLLUTION

Unfortunately, humans have damaged both the visibility of the sky and the quality of the air we breathe with our pollution, both light and air.

Light Pollution

When humans figured out how to harness electricity for artificial light, it was a remarkable feat. It advanced medicine, improved safety at night, and brightened our homes. Unfortunately though, it brought with it light pollution, artificial light that hinders our view of the night sky. Excessive fluorescent light from our cities and suburbs now drowns out our view of the stars. Light pollution can also alter our sleeping habits; confuse animal hibernation, feeding, and reproductive patterns; and upset bird migrations.[1]

During the day, haze diminishes our views of cities, scenic areas, and national parks and their skies. Haze forms when light encounters particles of pollution in the air, clouding out what we see by degrading clarity and color.[2] Perhaps you've seen the haze and smog that settle like a dirty cloud on cities like Los Angeles? Pretty sad, isn't it? This decreased visibility wasn't part of the original design of the skies.

Points *of* Air Pollution

CHEMICAL TRANSFORMATION
Ozone Destruction

Stratosphere

CHEMICAL TRANSFORMATION
Ozone Production

Troposphere

Free Troposphere

AIRCRAFT EMISSIONS

Long-range transport of aerosols and gases

CHEMICAL TRANSFORMATION
Deposition of pollutants

CLEAN OCEAN EVAPORATION

Boundary Layer

INDUSTRY

CITIES

Sulfur emission from ships

TRANSPORTATION

FARMING

WILDFIRES

DESERT DUST

BIOMASS BURNING

SHIPPING INDUSTRY

Air Pollution

The earth's atmosphere acts as a protective shield, blocking harmful UV sunrays and disintegrating meteors, while providing breathable air for all living things. The atmosphere is made up of life-sustaining gases: 78 percent nitrogen and 21 percent oxygen, with smaller amounts of carbon dioxide, helium, and neon. Air pollution occurs when these proportions are unnaturally altered or if toxic elements are added to the mix. Pollution has detrimental impacts on ecosystems and on human health.

Therefore, by being proponents of clean air, we support life.

One of the most common and problematic types of air pollution is particulate matter, which is a mixture of solid particles and air droplets light enough to float in the air. This includes dust, pollen, soot, or smoke, but the more troubling variety are made up of chemicals emitted from power plants and automobiles. Particulate matter enters our airways and infiltrates our lungs and can even be absorbed into our bloodstream. Other serious forms of gaseous air pollution are nitrous dioxide,

←

When solid and liquid particles—along with certain gases—become suspended in the air, they form air pollution. These gases and aerosols are created by everything from dust, pollen, and mold spores to car exhaust, factory farming, and wildfires. Most air pollution is caused by the burning of fossil fuels, transportation, agriculture, landfills, and exhaust from factories.

sulfur dioxide, and ozone. Carbon dioxide is also considered an air pollutant when its levels far exceed its natural limits, causing adverse effects across ecosystems and climate systems.

Most air pollution comes from transportation, followed by power plants, industrial furnaces, brick kilns, agriculture, and unregulated incineration of waste like plastics and batteries.[3] Cookstoves used by many rural communities are unsafe sources of air pollution in homes.

Exposure to air pollution can harm our respiratory, brain, and heart health. Particulate matter is especially problematic for pregnant women, placing them at a greater risk of having premature, underweight, or stillborn babies, disproportionately affecting African American mothers the most.[4] Particulate matter is also linked to dementia[5] and an increased incidence of cancer, including lung cancer.[6] Together, ambient (outdoor) and household air pollution contribute to around seven million premature deaths every year.[7] Therefore, by being proponents of clean air, we support life.

Mongolia Air Crisis

In 2018 Mongolia experienced a public health crisis when its capital city, Ulaanbaatar, reached air pollution levels more than one hundred times the acceptable limit. Massive amounts of people (half of the country's population) had moved to the city, as it was the only place with available jobs.[8] This population growth meant a major increase in the amount of cookstoves heating homes with the only affordable option for the community being coal.

The situation became so awful in Mongolia that children, whose lungs were still developing, were in and out of the intensive care ward at hospitals. Many suffered from coughing and pneumonia. The cityscape was continually covered in a cloud of smog, or smoke mixed with fog. But because the city was where the jobs were, many families couldn't move away.

The Clean Air Act

In the US, before 1970, cities across the country were disappearing behind clouds of thick smog. The Clean Air Act allowed the government to regulate air pollution emissions from sources like vehicles, power plants, and factories. It also addressed chemical pollutants that were damaging the atmosphere's ozone layer, which protects us from harmful UV rays from the sun, and aimed to reduce acid rain and improve air quality and visibility.

POLLUTION AND POVERTY

Most of the global population live in places where air quality fails to meet the guidelines of the World Health Organization.[9] People living in low- and middle-income countries are disproportionately affected by the burden of air pollution,[10] and urban areas are particularly vulnerable to dangerous levels of smog.

Today, people of color often suffer the most from air pollution and the illnesses and deaths that coincide with it.[11] Housing properties near polluting power plants and congested roadways are cheaper, and the residual effect of redlining—a now illegal systemic and racially discriminatory denial of financial services like mortgages—continues to bind families in pockets of poverty near high levels of air pollution. This adversely affects children whose playgrounds and schools are near industrial facilities, increasing asthmatic symptoms and attacks.

OUR RESPONSIBILITY

We may not be able to remove all light and air pollution—and as the global population grows, we'll have more challenges with air quality and visibility—but there is much we can do to limit and reverse the damage. It's time to support the solutions that keep our air cleaner and safer. With all the technological advances in energy options, we can keep the air cleaner for everyone. Clean, breathable air should be available to all. God has given us a great expanse in the heavens, and we have a responsibility to take care of and protect this priceless gift.

A BIBLICAL PERSPECTIVE

God sees every part of the planet that has gone wrong and is broken, including atmospheric issues. And He extends His mercy over our faults and failures in mishandling creation. In John 3:16, where it famously says, "for God so loved *the world, that he gave his only Son*" (emphasis added), the Greek word he uses, *kosmos*, refers to the entire universe. This means that God gave His Son not only to redeem you and

> **Clean, breathable air should be available to all.**

me but the whole earth as well. Do you love the world the way God does? Will you care for it as part of its redemption?

God's Creativity on Display

The astonishing views of the heavens above tell us about the Creator. The expanse of space is a blue-black tapestry with innumerable stars packed in clusters or spread out as luminous dust. Psalm 19:1 plainly states: "The heavens declare the glory of God, and the sky above proclaims his handiwork." We need to let the glory of God's natural lights in the sky reach more areas of our world. Clean air and clear views of the sky protect the witness of God's glory in creation for present and future generations to continue to be moved by a starry sky and wonder about the Maker of the cosmos.

God Is for Us

The skies and heavens aren't only beautiful—they're also perfectly planned, and they demonstrate to us that God is in control. The types of gases and their ratios in our atmosphere are just right for life to flourish. The originality of our planet's atmosphere suits the natural world it encases, as humans and plants share oxygen and carbon dioxide to live and breathe.

Outside the Milky Way, billions of other galaxies travel through the universe as it expands. The Hubble Space Telescope clocked one galaxy moving three million miles per hour away from us. God initiates and sustains the energy, gravity, and planetary forces of the cosmos. The universe expands, galaxies spin, and solar systems synchronize under His direction.

> The universe expands, galaxies spin, and solar systems synchronize under His direction.

In Psalm 46:10, God tells us to "be still, and know that I am God" (NIV). This verse stirs us to consider who's in control, who positioned Earth at just the right distance from the sun so the planet wouldn't burn up or freeze over. The God of the heavens and the Milky Way, the God who made Earth perfect for you and me to live—do you trust Him? In the commotion and confusion of life, we are invited to come before God in prayer and let Him still our anxieties about ecological crises. Use the skies to ponder your place on the earth, and ask God for direction on how to play your part in solving environmental problems like air pollution.

Make Time to Appreciate the Nighttime Sky

When was the last time you paused to look up and admire the stars, planets, and constellations? When we appreciate the atmosphere around us and the sky above us, we feel more connected to this part of creation and are motivated to take better care of it.

ENJOY STARGAZING AND ASTRONOMICAL VIEWS.

- ▶ Check out NASA's "Astronomy Picture of the Day" for different images of the cosmos viewed through modern technology. These pictures of galaxies, nebula, stars, planets, and other astrological sights inspire awe and wonder for our Creator and can be a wonderful way to start morning prayer time.

- ▶ Download stargazing or constellation apps like Star Walk. You can point your phone toward the sky and learn what stars and constellations you're looking at.

VISIT AN INTERNATIONAL DARK SKY PLACES (IDSP).

- ▶ Check out darksky.org to find an IDSP or protected area close to you to view a light pollution–free nighttime sky.

Improve and Track Air Quality

We can work with nature's God-designed ways of cleaning the air by planting greenery and trees either with a local environmental organization or in our own yards.

PLANT A TREE.

- ▸ Trees are natural air filters, removing air pollutants like sulfur dioxide, ozone, nitrogen oxides, and particulates.

KEEP UP-TO-DATE ON AIR QUALITY.

- ▸ Many cities have air-quality monitoring systems in place that continuously measure air pollutants, the results of which can be found online and on apps.

- ▸ Download the BreezoMeter app to track your exposure to air pollution. The app updates hourly and is available 24/7. Be in the know about air quality and share with your friends.

Reduce Light Pollution and Haze

Be intentional about the lights you use to improve our view of the nighttime sky and prevent confusion for migrating bird populations.

SWITCH IT OFF.

- ▸ Keep your lights off whenever possible to help reduce light pollution, save on your energy bill, and reduce your carbon footprint.

- ▸ Switch to LED lighting. This reduces illuminance while still providing sufficient visibility. It also reduces energy use and minimizes the emission of blue light, which is harmful to wildlife behavior, reproduction, and migration.

- ▸ Purchase light fixtures designed to reduce light pollution. Light designs should direct light toward the ground where it's needed and shield excess light from spilling over and up into the sky. Look for the International Dark-Sky Association (IDA) seal of approval when buying fixtures. You can also search for companies like Starry Night Lights, which sell low-pollution lighting.

- Support Dark-Sky initiatives in your area by speaking to your local representatives. Visit the IDA website for tips on how to support low light pollution standards in your area to reduce glare, light trespass, and skyglow.

Reduce Air Pollution

Many of our everyday activities affect the air we breathe. Our home, transportation, and consumer choices can help reduce pollution and keep communities healthier.

MAKE THE EV UPGRADE.

- Electric vehicles (EV) run solely on electricity and have zero tailpipe pollution. If you obtain electricity for your EV from wind or solar sources, manufacturing emissions are minuscule.
- EVs cost half the price to operate as gas-run cars,[12] and state and federal rebates and tax credits are available.
- Charging stations are popping up everywhere, in your everyday spots like Target and grocery store parking lots. Plus, many businesses have designated parking spaces for EVs—stress-free parking is reason enough!

GREEN YOUR CAR.

- Keep your car up to emissions standards. Routine car maintenance can catch issues that may be causing your car to pollute more. Regular tune-ups keep it running smoothly with fewer emissions.
- Check your tire pressure once a month. If the tire pressure is low, then more fuel will be burned.
- Reduce your vehicle's weight by removing unneeded items from inside your car or truck. Lightening your car's load will boost your fuel economy.

- One of the best ways to reduce air pollution is to cut back on how often you drive. By running multiple errands all at once, you can easily decrease your driving time. This is one of the simplest yet most important habits to change.

- Use a bike, public transit, and/or carpool. Organize a carpool with coworkers or classmates or search for local ride-sharing services.

USE WATER-BASED PAINTS AND CLEANERS.

- Chemical-based paints and personal-care and cleaning products can have volatile organic compounds (VOC), common air contaminants.

- Buy cleaning products labeled with low or zero VOCs. Add this as a note to your shopping list to help you remember.

Advocate for Policy Solutions and Support Nonprofits Working to Decrease Air Pollution

When air pollution is beyond the immediate control of individuals, we can support policies and provisions that work to reduce emissions and pollution and encourage movement toward cleaner options. Many organizations with expertise in air pollution issues are doing beneficial work in communities at home and abroad.

ADVOCATE FOR EMISSION REDUCTIONS AND CLEAN ENERGY SOLUTIONS.

- Call or write a letter to your representative to let them know air pollution standards and reductions in your area are important to you. Visit www.usa.gov/elected-officials to learn how to contact your representative.

- Include topics like transitioning to clean technologies that reduce smokestack emissions, improved and increased incentives for EVs both for residents and public transportation, incentives to promote the incorporation of more renewable power sources (solar, wind, hydropower) into the electric grid for utility uses at home, and incentives for local small-scale renewable energy options like at-home rooftop solar power generation.

SUPPORT ENVIRONMENTAL NONPROFITS.

- ▸ **Earthjustice** is a nonprofit law organization that works to protect public health from air pollution and to advance clean energy solutions.

- ▸ **WISE Women's Clean Cookstoves Project** educates women in Nigeria about clean cookstoves, with trainings, financing, and purchasing insights.

- ▸ **Project Drawdown** and the **Global Peace Foundation** both have projects focused on improved clean cookstove accessibility for global communities.

- ▸ **Clean Air Task Force** is a nonprofit that leads successful campaigns to reduce air pollution in the US.

CHAPTER FIVE

WOODLANDS

Our Disappearing Forests

The earth brought forth vegetation, plants yielding seed according to their own kinds, and trees bearing fruit in which is their seed, each according to its kind. And God saw that it was good.

GENESIS 1:12

THE FORESTS OF THE EARTH SUPPORT AN AMAZING ASSORTMENT of trees, each suited to location and climate. The leaf shapes vary—oval, heart, lobed, spiked—and combine to form distinct canopies around the planet. Boreal forests are adapted to harsh, cold temperatures and snowfall. From an aerial view, their canopies are sparse, with pointed tops of conifer trees that triangulate down, the needle-covered branches lengthening toward the bottom of the trunk. The broadleaf forests have thick bundles of leaves from oaks, redwoods, and maples, with canopies that look undeniably like bunches of broccoli. Toward the equator, tropical climates create an oasis for rainforests whose dense canopies grow to soaring heights.

> It's a playground for God's most raucous and curious creatures on the planet.

The humidity and moisture of the rainforest yield wild harvests of exotic plant life. Big, brazen, and beautiful flowers attract iridescent hummingbirds and resplendent butterflies. Venus fly traps snap their jaws on insect prey. Vegetation of all shades of green—lime, forest, sage, and olive—with some leaves as big as kites, tumbles and parades across the terrain. Jaguars climb trees to stalk their prey or rest on a bough. Monkeys scale the towering trunks and swing from branches and vines. The forest is overwhelmingly alive. It's a playground for God's most raucous and curious creatures on the planet. And it's disappearing at an alarming rate.

DEFORESTATION

As the world's population continues to grow, we use and destroy more and more forests to meet our needs for food, material goods, and space for homes and buildings. Known as *deforestation*, forests rapidly disappear when we fail to replant trees and restore the woodlands. Humans have wiped out more than 30 percent of all the planet's forests since preindustrial times, and we've degraded and fragmented swaths of what's left.[1]

Wisely managed tree loss can be a good tool for foresters to promote healthy growth and regeneration for the forest as a whole.[2] Forests are most resilient when they have trees of diverse age, size, and species present. And there are responsible ways to carry out logging activities for wood and paper products. Unfortunately, though, many trees are illegally cut down in ways that destroy entire forest lands for decades. And tropical rainforests are threatened by deforestation to a serious degree. In 2019 a football field worth of trees were lost every six seconds in the tropics.[3]

> Humans have wiped out more than 30 percent of all the planet's forests since preindustrial times, and we've degraded and fragmented swaths of what's left.

A major method behind tropical deforestation is known as *slash-and-burn agriculture*. Small-scale farmers cut down forests and then burn them to grow crops in the soils fertilized by the ashes. This technique is highly unsustainable because the land stops producing crops in just a few years. The farm is then abandoned, new forest space burned, and the cycle continues. Forests are also commonly cleared by fire in Southeast Asia, tropical Africa, and the Americas for oil palm plantations, as demand for palm oil for many everyday products continues to increase.

There's a great tension here with the destruction of forests and the jobs and products the industry provides. Many workers are under the poverty line and lack access to other options. Globally, one in four people rely on forests for their livelihoods.[4] About one-fifth of the world's rural population (750 million people) live in forests, including 60 million indigenous people.[5]

THE IMPORTANCE OF THE RAINFORESTS

Rainforests are especially precious to the planet because they house more biodiversity within their borders than any other area on earth. The Amazon rainforest is home to more than six thousand tree types,[6] which create rich and vibrant habitats for several million species.[7] It is the largest remaining portion of humid tropical forest; nearly two-thirds of it is located in Brazil. However, in the past fifty years, we've eradicated about 17 percent of the Amazonian rainforest, mostly due to forest clearing for cattle ranching.[8]

We can't afford to keep cutting down forests at a rate and in ways in which they can't be restored. Clearing forests reduces humidity and rainfall, which are vital for agricultural areas like Brazil. Larger ecosystems, like rainforests, may be forced to undergo regime shifts (an abrupt change from one type of biome to another) suddenly, like falling dominoes.[9] There's a tipping point, long foreseen by scientists, in which the Amazon rainforest would begin to transition into a dry savanna if the total deforested area surpasses 40 percent.[10] Currently, this catastrophic shift is estimated to take place in less than thirty years if trends in forest loss continue.[11] Our rainforests help regulate our global climate and influence agriculture yields

> Removing huge areas of natural forests is like cutting off a body's connection to a vital organ; it throws off the whole system.

across continents. Removing huge areas of natural forests is like cutting off a body's connection to a vital organ; it throws off the whole system.

A WAY FORWARD

A healthy planet needs thriving forests. Replanting and regeneration of forests across the world will help with air pollution, climate regulation, water quality, and more.

We can implement foresting techniques that are less harmful to the earth and allow for trees to grow back successfully and forests to recover, while at the same time considering the livelihoods of farmers and foresters. Our forests clean our air, filter our water, regulate our life-generating carbon and water cycles, provide food and medicines, strengthen our soil, and provide shelter for a wonderful abundance of plants and animals. This, along with their natural beauty, makes them a valuable part of God's creation!

→

The carbon cycle is the biogeochemical process by which carbon is exchanged and is critical for maintaining a stable carbon balance and climate. It consists of these steps: carbon moves from the air to plants (in photosynthesis), from plants to animals, from plants and animals to soil (through decomposition), from living things and fossil fuels to the atmosphere, and from the atmosphere to the ocean.

Elements *of the* Forest Carbon Cycle

CARBON DIOXIDE (CO$_2$) IN ATMOSPHERE

COMBUSTION OF FUELS

Industry

Fossil fuels (oil, gas, coal)

DIFFUSION

PHOTOSYNTHESIS

Plants

CELL RESPIRATION

Animals

DISSOLVED CO$_2$

BICARBONATES

CARBONATES IN SEDIMENTS

DECOMPOSERS:
Fungi, earthworms, microbes

A BIBLICAL PERSPECTIVE

The Tree of Life has a final startling cameo when the Scriptures are wrapping up in Revelation. The new heaven and new earth have come, and there by the river of the water of life is the Tree of Life, and the "leaves of the tree are for the healing of the nations" (Revelation 22:2 NIV). It's a place where heaven and earth are in harmony again, and God gives nourishment to the entire world through a tree.[12] The spiritual and physical nature of this tree remains a mystery to us now, but we can marvel at the role trees play in the biblical accounts of grand-scale redemption. How masterful are the plans of our redeemer God!

God's Plan for Trees

In the passage from Genesis 1, which opened this chapter, after God created vegetation and trees, God said *it is good*. Trees were a part of the creation story and a part of creation's worship. As Christians, we're accustomed to worship. But did you know that in the new heaven and new earth, the trees will praise, too, in their own arboreal way? Isaiah 44:23 exhorts every tree in the forest to "break forth into singing" because the Lord has redeemed His people. "For you shall go out in joy and be led forth in peace; the mountains and the hills before you shall break forth

> **The new heaven and new earth have come, and there by the river of the water of life is the Tree of Life.**

into singing, and all the trees of the field shall clap their hands"
(Isaiah 55:12).

Jesus and Trees

Have you ever thought about the fact that, before His ministry
began at age thirty, Jesus worked with the same type of wooden
material that would make up the cross? He
sawed, sanded, whittled, and carved slabs
of tree. He would've hammered and nailed
pieces together. The feel of wood was very
familiar to Him in life, and it's what He'd
voluntarily lean back against during His
death. All along, Jesus, as God, knew that
He would one day use the timber material
of His earthly career to bring about our

**It's a place where
heaven and earth
are in harmony
again, and God
gives nourishment
to the entire world
through a tree.**

great salvation. What a humble Savior, worthy of our worship. He
interacted with nature and trees in a meaningful way—in both life
and in death—to serve others.

Trees in the Bible

All throughout Scripture, God uses trees to communicate His
redemption story. In Genesis 2, Adam and Eve were banished from
the garden of Eden after eating from the forbidden Tree of the
Knowledge of Good and Evil. But there was another tree in the
middle of the garden, the Tree of Life, through which God offered
eternal nourishment and immortality. Our sin lost us connection

But there was another tree in the middle of the garden, the Tree of Life, through which God offered eternal nourishment and immortality.

with this tree, but Jesus came to earth and claimed to be the source of eternal life, the true vine with many branches (John 15:5). In fact, He compared the kingdom to a large tree that grows and spreads out "so that the birds of the air come and make nests in its branches" (Matthew 13:32).

Learn About and Engage with Your Local Forests

The best way to learn about the value of forests is to get to know the ones in your area. You rest under the shade of trees; you breathe the clean air they actively filter. You hear the twigs snap and leaves rustle, and you watch insects, birds, and other creatures live within the forest's shelter. Experiencing your nearby forests will help you maintain gratitude for these important habitats.

FIND A TREE FIELD GUIDE.

- Leaf forms, bark types, and other features offer clues for tree identification. A field guide provides pictures and illustrations of each tree species and their unique attributes.

- Take a field guide with you to a forest or your backyard and compare the different features of each tree.

JOIN LOCAL RESTORATION OR TREE-PLANTING PROJECTS.

- Look up efforts in your area to uphold and protect the health of your forests. There may be tree-planting events or invasive-species removal projects. The Nature Conservancy is a good place to start.

CHECK OUT GLOBAL FOREST WATCH ONLINE.

- This online forest monitoring system led by the World Resources Institute uses satellite imagery to detect changes in tree cover in near–real time around the planet.

Ensure Your Rainforest Products are Sourced from Ethical Supply Chains

Slash-and-burn deforestation and other unsustainable agricultural methods account for nearly 80 percent of deforestation in tropical and subtropical areas.[13] Increase the demand for ethically and sustainably sourced goods from rainforest products through your purchasing power.

COFFEE

Around 61 percent of coffee producers receive prices that are under the cost of production for their coffee beans.[14] Fair trade coffee uses third-party evaluations and certifications to ensure price and environmental standards are met. Direct trade involves coffee companies engaging directly with specific farms so there's transparency in the supply chain.

▸ Look for the Fairtrade-certified label or ask your local coffee shops about their sourcing methods. You'll enjoy that hot bean juice even more knowing it left the land and farmers happy.

▸ Support coffee brands that have good practices, such as Café Mam, Stumptown Coffee Roasters, Conscious Coffees, Pura Vida Coffee, and Rise Up Coffee Roasters.

▸ Consider shade-grown coffee, which means the beans were grown under a canopy or other vegetation. This method is beneficial to the land and wildlife, especially birds. Look for the Smithsonian Migratory Bird Center's Bird Friendly certification, which signifies the coffee is shade-grown as well as organic.

COCOA

Cocoa can be cultivated under a forest canopy, but many cocoa farmers are cutting down forests to grow a greater amount in the sun. This degrades soil, wipes out wildlife habitat, and creates more chemical runoff that pollutes streams and waterways.[15] The cocoa industry has also been guilty of child labor, forced labor, and gender inequality.

- Look for chocolate certified by the Rainforest Alliance, which engages with small-scale cocoa farmers to encourage returning to shade-grown cocoa. Let's make sure our chocolate is as ethical as it is tasty.

BEEF CATTLE

Swaths of rainforest in Brazil are being cleared to make space for grazing land for cattle.

- Find out where fast-food restaurants source their beef and avoid any that use beef from Brazil.
- Try alternative beef options like the Beyond Burger, a plant-based burger that looks, cooks, and tastes like meat. You won't believe it 'til you try it!

PALM OIL

Palm oil comes from a rainforest plant, and it's found in food products, cosmetics, shampoos, soaps, and many other everyday items. Rainforests in Indonesia are being replaced by oil palm plantations at an alarming rate to meet demand. As a result, habitats for orangutans are being wiped out, pushing them toward extinction.

- Palm oil production provides livelihoods for more than three million smallholder farmers.[16] Support these communities by building their capacity and providing training on sustainable methods for palm oil production—which is key to slowing the rate of deforestation.
- The Roundtable on Sustainable Palm Oil (RSPO) met in 2004, which led to commitments from multinational companies to trace supply chains and purchase only palm oil that's been sustainably harvested.
- Look for the RSPO certification or the Rainforest Alliance certification on palm oil products. Visit the RSPO website for an expansive list of certified sustainable palm oil products.

Make Daily Choices that Conserve Wood Products

Decisions about the furniture and paper you purchase can lessen unnecessary and unsustainable deforestation. The United States, Europe, and Australia have passed laws in recent years to prohibit the importation of illegally sourced and traded wood products.

MAKE INFORMED DECISIONS ABOUT PAPER AND WOOD PRODUCTS.

- ▸ Choose products that come from sustainable harvesting practices, which replant and restore forests in the process.

- ▸ Purchase products that display certifications from groups like the Forest Stewardship Council (FSC) and the Sustainable Forestry Initiative (SFI).

- ▸ Conserve the amount of paper you use, and reuse it when you can. Avoid consumable paper products like paper plates and cups. Even if the paper is sustainably sourced, try not to waste this resource that ultimately came from a tree.

- ▸ Always recycle your paper. In the US, 38 percent of the fiber used to make new paper products comes from recycled paper.[17]

- ▸ Purchase paper made from recycled materials when it's an option. Inspire your classmates or coworkers with your tree-friendly notebooks and business supplies!

- ▸ Limit your online purchases to reduce excessive amounts of cardboard and other paper. When given the option, choose to ship items together. Or take a trip to the store and enjoy the novelty of shopping in person.

BUY SUSTAINABLY SOURCED FURNITURE.

- ▸ The furniture and flooring of our homes and offices may be made of wood from tropical forests, which contain valuable timber resources like mahogany, rosewood, and sandalwood.[18] Find out if your purchases are sustainably sourced.

▸ Support furniture brands that use recycled materials and certified sustainable timber products and uphold high standards on fair labor and trade. Check out reclaimed furniture on Etsy, Medley Home, VivaTerra, West Elm, Simbly, Burrow, The Citizenry, ABC Carpet & Home, Sabai, and Crate & Barrel (FSC-certified furniture collection).

▸ Find artisan carpenters in your area for original furniture pieces from recycled "trash" wood or certified timber. A coffee table made from reclaimed wood is the height of environmentally chic.

Support Nonprofits and Projects Working to Reverse Deforestation

▸ **Plant with Purpose** works with communities to reverse deforestation through projects in agroforestry, reforestation, and tree nurseries.

▸ **Amazon Watch** has been working for decades to protect the rainforest and expand the rights and sustainable practices of indigenous peoples in the Amazon Basin.

▸ **One Trillion Trees** is a joint initiative between nonprofits, governments, and businesses, with the goal to conserve and restore one trillion trees by 2030.

CHAPTER SIX

SOIL

Agriculture's Active Ingredient

"Unless a kernel of wheat falls to the ground and dies, it remains only a single seed. But if it dies, it produces many seeds."

JOHN 12:24 (NIV)

HOW OFTEN DO YOU THINK ABOUT WHERE YOUR FOOD COMES from, or the soil that helped it grow? Farms are living ecosystems—full of plants, animals, soil, water, and air working together in a balance that upholds the land's integrity and longevity. They flourish when biodiversity is strong, and harvests are plentiful when all parts of the natural system are present. A key ingredient to a farm's health is its soil.

Soil vs. Dirt

What's the difference between dirt and soil? Dirt is made by the weathering of rocks over time, as wind and water slowly break down rocks into sand, clay, and silt. Soil is dirt plus water, air, and bits of decomposed plants and animals (organic matter). Mushrooms, slime molds, fungi, and bacteria in the soil all work to help decay deceased things and release their nutrients for reuse. These natural fertilizers are the champions of soil health.

Did you know that a single teaspoon of soil is alive with billions of microscopic organisms? "Living soil" is foundational to productive farmlands and helps convert nutrients for plants, build soil structure, and improve water absorption. Unfortunately, we have severely degraded the earth's soil, with a third of it lost to intensive agriculture. The United Nations (UN) estimates that twenty-four billion tons of fertile soil is lost each year.[1]

UNSUSTAINABLE AGRICULTURAL PRACTICES

In the past fifty years industrial agriculture techniques have doubled agricultural productivity and fed a population that has also doubled in the same amount of time.[2] Industrial agriculture is large-scale, mechanized intensive production of crops and livestock. These types of farms typically only produce one type of crop (like rice, maize, or wheat), and the land is also doused with chemical fertilizers and pesticides. Meat production happens in confined animal feeding operations (CAFO), where the livestock live in crammed conditions that are prime for the spread of disease, and therefore they're heavily vaccinated and given a surplus of antibiotics, leading to antibiotic-resistant bacteria. All of these methods have been applied to maximize crop yields and meat production to feed people, plus make a profit.

However, these methods come with a steep environmental price, which threatens the ability of the land to continually produce enough for everyone. Monocultures strip a land of its biodiversity and its natural ways of regenerating itself for sustained fruitfulness. Plowing, overcropping, and hedge and tree removal cause rain and wind to wash away soil. Around the planet, this soil is eroded ten to forty times faster than it's replaced, depleting cropland close to the size of England yearly.[3]

> Around the planet, this soil is eroded ten to forty times faster than it's replaced, depleting cropland close to the size of England yearly.

These agricultural practices lead to exhausted soil in need of, unfortunately, more artificial fertilizer. At times, in areas of the Baltic Sea and Chesapeake Bay, dead fish float up and cover the water's surface. A gross, smelly, and sad situation! This happens when excessive fertilizer leaches into waterways and causes an overgrowth of algae, creating "dead zones" where oxygen runs out and fish suffocate. Many bodies of water around the world suffer from dead zones, harming fish harvests and affecting fishing communities.

THE FOOD AND WASTE PROBLEM

Healthy soil is one problem; food shortage is another. The planet produces an abundance of food, and yet around 690 million people went hungry in 2019.[4] In the same year nearly a quarter of children under five years of age were stunted, lacking the vitamins and minerals needed for a healthy diet (known as malnutrition).[5] Farmers produce enough food to feed around 10 billion people, which is 1.5 times the global population.[6] However, we waste about a third of it.[7] Imagine throwing out a third of your paycheck or letting a third of the food in your refrigerator go bad. Food waste is a serious global problem. It's not about having enough food for everyone; rather, it's about getting nutritious food to everyone who needs it.

Most people who experience chronic hunger live in extreme poverty in developing countries where food shortages occur. As much as 40 percent of food grown in some regions becomes spoilage. Smallholder farmers often lack adequate storage facilities to prevent this, and they don't always have the roads and highways to safely transport the food in time.

SUSTAINABLE AGRICULTURE

The problems of soil depletion and food waste for a growing population can be mitigated with sustainable agriculture. This includes farming methods that allow us to grow crops and tend livestock without depleting the land's ability to continue to produce more food for our future needs. We are learning how to work with nature to keep the soil healthy and the land fertile and productive on our farms and in community and home gardens. This sets up current and future generations to continually harvest the earth's plants in

Global Food Production *and* Waste

$1 TRILLION DOLLARS' WORTH OF FOOD IS LOST OR WASTED EVERY YEAR.

IF EVEN 25% OF THE FOOD CURRENTLY LOST OR WASTED COULD BE SAVED, IT COULD EASILY FEED 870 MILLION HUNGRY PEOPLE IN THE WORLD.

UNITED STATES

In the United States alone, $48.3 billion is thrown away each year. Overall losses are $90–100 billion per year.

EUROPE

The food currently wasted in Europe—about 6.7 million tonnes—could feed 200 million people.

ASIA

In Asia, around 23 million tonnes of food cereals, 12 million tonnes of fruits, and 21 million tonnes of vegetables are lost each year.

LATIN AMERICA

In Latin America the food lost or wasted could feed 300 million people.

AFRICA

In Africa, losses can reach up to 50% for some less-hardy crops, such as fruits, vegetables, and root crops.

INDIA

An estimated 580 billion rupees (nearly $8 billion) is wasted each year in India, in agricultural produce.

AUSTRALIA

In Australia, an estimated $10.5 billion was spent on items thrown away (more than $5,000 per capita per year).

a way that allows the land to regenerate itself naturally.

The challenge of the future is to adapt our food systems toward agricultural practices that support soil health and create secure transport of food to everyone. We need to be less reliant on monocultures of cereal crops like wheat, corn, and grain (most of which goes to feeding livestock), and focus on harvesting nutritious vegetables, fruits, and legumes more locally when possible. Excessive use of fertilizers and pesticides and frequent tilling disrupts and damages the living organisms in soil and exacerbates erosion. Shifting to sustainable and organic practices—including practices and principles such as permaculture, rewilding, and regenerative farming—is vital for the growth of long-lasting productive farmlands and nutritious foods to feed and nourish our growing population.

> The challenge of the future is to adapt our food systems toward agricultural practices that support soil health and create secure transport of food to everyone.

←

An estimated 690 million people are hungry in the world—primarily in Asia and Africa—with the main problems being massive global food waste and poor distribution. A third of the food produced—around 1.3 billion tonnes—is either lost or wasted every year. About 35 percent are losses at the farm level, and another 26 percent are lost at the retail sector. Supermarkets, however, lost only about 1 percent.[8]

A WAY FORWARD

How can we balance the seemingly competing needs to protect our soil and feed the earth's population? This will take creativity from leaders and institutions around the world, but it's not out of reach. The good news for you and me is that there are small, actionable steps we can all take to both protect our land and provide for our neighbor.

A BIBLICAL PERSPECTIVE

As Christians, we should model ourselves after the disciples and give generously. This might mean sending and serving food to those in need, helping communities grow healthy fruits and vegetables, or supporting farms with practices that care well for the land, its soil, and, in turn, its people. In a sense, we've been given back the gardening tools of Eden: God's presence and practical insights into the workings of a flourishing natural world. We're equipped to steward the earth, with the richness and vibrancy of Eden as our inspiration.

Made from Dirt and Made to Care for It

As we see in Genesis, God fashioned us out of dirt, and yet we were made in the image of God. We are connected both to the earth and to heaven. After the Fall of man, for the very first time humans experienced a broken relationship with the soil (Genesis 3:19). But

God commanded us to work the land, and even now, we're still charged with its care. When we repent of selfish attitudes and actions and humble ourselves, God promises to hear us and heal the land (2 Chronicles 7:14). When we care for the earth, we ultimately participate in God's original design for us—made from dust yet positioned in heavenly places where Christ is seated (Ephesians 2:6). While we can't reach perfection while here on Earth, we can walk with God in our current landscapes and honor Him in how we cultivate the earth, while praying how Jesus taught us to pray: "On earth as it is in heaven."

God's Redemption Plan for Soil

In nature we constantly see death producing life, decaying materials at the bottom of the food chain turning into life's new beginnings. This circle of life starts and ends with soil. When we disrespect the land and don't honor its limits, we can strip it of nutrients and steal away its ability to flourish and produce. This should alarm us, because as we've seen, the results for our global populations can be devastating.

But as Christians, we know that God redeems. The Lord says: "Behold, I am making all things new" (Revelation 21:5). God reconciled to Himself "all things, whether things on earth or things in heaven" (Colossians 1:20 NIV). *All* things are reconciled to God through Christ,

> **All things are reconciled to God through Christ, including creation and the land.**

including creation and the land. If we fail to grasp the good news that creation—even soil—will also be redeemed and made new, then we're underestimating God's plan in a colossal way. When we learn to revere the earth the way Scripture does, and as we grasp that God plans to redeem every broken bit of it, our love for both God and nature must increase. He is good and faithful—*even to dirt*!

A Calling to Feed the Hungry

Jesus cared greatly about people's physical needs for food while He walked on the earth. He had compassion on a crowd of five thousand people and fed them with a miraculously small number of fish and loaves. Scripture tells us in 1 John that if we have the world's goods and see a brother or sister in need and don't make the effort to help them, then we lie and don't practice the truth (3:17).

God uses His people to fulfill His will and take care of His flock, especially those who are in need. In Acts 11:29, the disciples sent provisions to the brothers and sisters living in Judea to support them with the food they would need through the famine. We also must face the reality that people at home and around the globe, including ourselves, can be vulnerable to food insecurity—whether due to famine, food shortage, or natural disaster—and it's our collective responsibility to find the ways forward to cultivate the earth and distribute food to every hungry person.

Understand what *Organic* and *Local* Mean

We're often encouraged to buy food that's better for the environment and people, but the descriptors can get confusing. It's helpful to know what to look for. Buy both local and organic food when possible, but the best is to watch for regenerative agricultural products.

ORGANIC

- For food to be labeled and certified as organic, it must meet USDA standards, which include criteria for soil and water quality, animal raising practices, pest and weed control, restrictions on chemical additives, and prohibition of antibiotics and growth hormones. Organic food is likely the most sustainable option at your local supermarket.

LOCAL

- At local farmers markets, enquire about farmers' organic practices. Because the certification process can be expensive, small farmers may be using sustainable practices without getting certified.

- Local doesn't always mean organic (and vice versa), but it should be fresher and likely more nutritious.

- Join a community-supported agriculture (CSA) or crop-sharing program that allows you to connect with the food producers and subscribe to the harvest of particular farms.

Prevent Food Waste

Every year Americans throw out nearly 80 billion pounds of food, equivalent to 1,000 Empire State Buildings![9] That's about 219 pounds of waste per person and nearly 40 percent of the US food supply. By making changes to our buying and eating habits, we can better steward and appreciate the gift of food.

UNDERSTAND EXPIRATION LABELS.

- ▸ "Best if used by" describes a state of food quality that may not be the highest in taste, while still being safe to consume. "Use by" is for perishable foods that have a time limit for food safety.[10]

COMPOST.

- ▸ Compost works wonders for soil health in your home garden, as mulch in your yard, and/or for houseplants. Do not compost diseased plants, dog or cat manure, coal or charcoal ash, dairy products (e.g., butter, milk, sour cream, yogurt) and eggs (except eggshells), fats, grease, lard or oils, meat or fish bones and scraps, black walnut tree leaves or twigs, or yard trimmings treated with chemical pesticides. One trick to prevent odor is to store your compost items in a bag in the freezer.

FREEZE OR REPURPOSE FOOD.

- ▸ Save food (like meat and bread) before it perishes by freezing it for later.
- ▸ Freeze fruit, spinach, or kale and use it to make smoothies later. Turn your vegetables into stock or juice them. Be proactive and creative!
- ▸ Learn how to make fruit jam, how to pickle, or how to store vegetables in jars.

- There are programs that will sell produce with discoloring, bumps, or irregular shapes (which supermarkets often throw out even though it's still edible). Look into Imperfect Foods and Misfits Market.

Support Farms Using Regenerative and Sustainable Agricultural Practices

If land is overused and eroded, soil loses the necessary ingredients for life. We can pack soil with artificial fertilizer to make up for it, but the microbes and fungi aren't replaceable. Purchase your produce from farms that incorporate restorative and sustainable practices to regenerate the land for further production.

LEARN ABOUT A FARM'S UNIQUE JOURNEY TO SUSTAINABILITY.

- There's not a single prescription for every farm, but depending on each one's location and climate, sustainable techniques and regenerative practices can be incorporated.

- Regenerative farms harness the natural cycle of the ecology of the land to allow for regeneration, creating healthy (microbe vibrant) soil and long-term productivity.

- Visit farms near you and learn about their sustainable initiatives. Some regenerative and sustainable practices you can ask about include rotating crop diversity, planting cover crops, no-till or reduced till methods, livestock integration, agroforestry, and buffer zones.

Support Local and International Organizations

Learn about food issues in your area, and look for ways to help communities get nutritional food through means that keep their lands productive.

VOLUNTEER OR INITIATE FOOD CHARITY EFFORTS AT CHURCH.

- ▸ Churches often have or support food programs like soup kitchens or food pantries. Volunteer at one or get one started in your local area.

INITIATE A NEIGHBORHOOD GARDEN.

- ▸ Reach out to your neighbors to see if there's interest in growing food together and start a committee with the widest range of talent possible (green thumbs, carpenters, etc.). It's a great opportunity to build community!

- ▸ Decide on a site. If it's not in someone's yard, you will likely need to get permission from a local governing body and retrieve any relevant lease agreements or insurance policies from landowners.

- ▸ Research crops that do well in your local climate and design your garden. Share your produce with neighbors or donate part of the harvest to a food pantry.

SUPPORT ORGANIZATIONS.

- ▸ **Growing Hope Globally** is a faith-based nonprofit that works on issues of food insecurity with churches and communities to end world hunger.

- ▸ **Echo: Hope Against Hunger** is a faith-based organization that equips small-scale farmers and their families with sustainable agricultural practices.

Choose Sustainable Fashion Over Fast Fashion

You may not think about farms when you purchase clothing, but our fabrics contain agricultural products, like cotton, flax, or hemp. These raw-textile materials require land, natural resources, and labor.

WAKE UP TO THE FAST-FASHION WASTE PROBLEM.

- In 2018, the US generated about 13,000 tons of clothing and footwear textiles, with more than 9,000 ending up in landfills.[11]

- Fast fashion uses excessive nutrients from fertilizers, and chemicals for production pollute rivers and streams. Chemicals are needed to dye and finish fabric.

- About 700 gallons of water are used to make a single T-shirt[12]— equivalent to the amount of water for one person to drink eight cups a day for 3.5 years.

- Fast fashion has been exposed in the past for violations of human rights with poor working conditions and child labor.

SHOP WITH SUSTAINABLE FASHION IN MIND.

- Look for certification labels, such as Fair Wear Foundation, Fair Trade Certified, Ethical Trading Initiative, and Certified B Corporation, for companies that follow sustainable and ethical practices.

- Always wash your new clothes and check for clothes with the chemical content certification label: OEKO-TEX, GOTS, or BLUESIGN.

- Buy secondhand clothing from thrift shops and consignment stores.

- Check out these ethical and sustainable brands: Everlane, Redemption, Pact, Alternative Apparel, Mate, Warp + Weft, Cariuma, Allbirds, Outerknown, Patagonia, and others.

CHAPTER SEVEN

POLLINATORS

Our Overlooked Helpers

Now John wore a garment of camel's hair and a leather belt
around his waist, and his food was locusts and wild honey.

MATTHEW 3:4

DO BEES COME TO MIND WHEN YOU USE A DOLLOP OF HONEY?
How about when you add almonds to a salad or avocado on toast?
More than two-thirds of the world's agricultural crops count on
pollinators, which makes them essential to our environment.[1] We
have pollinators to thank whenever we enjoy food staples like
potatoes, carrots, bell peppers, squash, avocados, apples, blueber-
ries, lemons, and many others. The fruits and seeds produced from
pollination, as well as the insects them-
selves, make up a substantial portion of the
diets of other animals, and without these
insects, the food web would break down
across ecosystems.

> Think of the
> wonders we
> would lose in the
> world without this
> complex, mutual
> "friendship"
> between the plants
> and insects.

Around 80 percent of all flowering
plants depend on insects and other animals for pollination.[2] We wouldn't have
the variety of flowers that beautify our
planet without pollinators. Think of the

wonders we would lose in the world without this complex, mutual "friendship" between the plants and insects. Unfortunately, pollinators are in serious decline due to habitat loss, pesticide use, and introduced diseases—and they need our help to recover.

THE DECLINE OF INSECTS

Declining trends in insect populations have set off alarms in the scientific community, sounding out calls for protection and recovery of pollinator species. In Germany, flying insects in nature reserves decreased by 75 percent from 1989 to 2016.[3] More than 40 percent of insect species are threatened with extinction.[4] Findings like these triggered talk of an "insect apocalypse," with the rising fear that if we lose our bugs, crop devastation and ecosystem collapse across the world would follow. But as with much in nature, the future trajectory is not certain or always clear.

To predict global trends for insects, scientists may use models that take data from a handful of locations and then apply or project those statistics to other unstudied areas. This can oversimplify the actual numbers—one studied region may not be representative of the rest of the planet, for example. Insect populations fluctuate widely over time and space, and it's challenging to discern long-term trends. Even so, land-dwelling insects have declined in abundance every decade. This is troubling on a global scale and enough to motivate us to do something to protect and support our valuable insects.

Bees

Every spring, large trucks travel up the coast of California, delivering about one million hives of honeybees to almond orchards to let them pollinate the crops. This managed pollination effort is the largest in the world, and it's a response to the collapse of natural bee colonies across the United States.

Globally, the number of different kinds of bee species is estimated at 20,000, with around 3,600 in the US and Canada alone. However, many species of bumblebees and honeybees are declining

What Is Pollination?

In the pollination of flowers, pollen is transferred via the stamen (the pollen-producing part of a flower) from the anther (the part of the stamen where pollen is produced) to the stigma (the part of the pistil, or ovule-producing part of a flower, where pollen germinates), either in the same plant (self-pollination) or a different one (cross-pollination), which ensures viable fruit and seed production. Insects, birds, and bats all play a role in the transfer of pollen, but insects are by far the most active and exhibit vital, interdependent relationships with plants. Flowers allure insects with their vibrant colors and sweet-smelling, sugary nectar, and they are structurally adapted to the insects' mouths. Some insects have special tools and abilities to access the pollen or nectar, like long, rolled "tongues" that uncoil and reach the nectar at the deep base of tubular flowers. The blue-banded bees of Australia, along with many carpenter bees and bumble bees, buzz and vibrate to release pollen, a fascinating trick called "buzz pollination."

across North America. The rusty patched bumblebee was placed on the endangered species list when its numbers dwindled dangerously low. Honeybee colonies in the US declined by 3.5 million over six decades (in 1947 the record high was six million).[5] Although they receive less attention, wild bees are even more endangered. Over half of the native bee species disappeared in the Midwest during the last century.[6]

Butterflies and Moths

Butterflies and moths are also experiencing noteworthy declines. In North America, the iconic monarch butterfly used to frequently flutter about our yards. Now their orange wings outlined with black patterns and white dots are rarely seen. In the East, they're critically imperiled, and in the West, they're vulnerable to extinction.[7] Efforts are underway to build "monarch waystations," stopping points with food and shelter, along their impressive three-thousand-mile migration to Mexico.

Bats

Though not part of the insect family of pollinators we've been focusing on, bats are important nocturnal pollinators in tropical and desert climates. Most bat species that feed off of and help pollinate flowers live in Africa, Southeast Asia, and the Pacific Islands. More than three hundred different kinds of fruits depend on bats for pollination, including mangoes, bananas, and guavas.[8] In North America, some bat species, which also eat millions of mosquitoes,

The Importance *of* Pollinators

WHO ARE THE POLLINATORS?

Insects (such as ants, bees, butterflies, and flies), animals (such as birds, bats, reptiles, squirrels, rodents, and monkeys)—and even people.

ARE THERE OTHER WAYS TO POLLINATE?

Yes—wind often carries pollen and some flowers self-pollinate.

WHICH IS THE BIGGEST POLLINATOR?

Bees. They top the pollination success charts by far, and in 2010, honeybees contributed to 19 billion dollars in pollinated crops.

WHY ARE POLLINATORS IMPORTANT?

More than half of our food source depends on them.

WHAT KINDS OF FOOD RELY ON POLLINATION?

Most of our fruits (from apples to tomatoes), nuts and seeds (from almonds to sesame), spices and seasonings (from anise to vanilla), dairy products (our cows rely on pollinated alfalfa), and even coffee and chocolate!

HOW MANY PLANTS OVERALL RELY ON POLLINATION?

More than 75 percent of flowering plants rely on pollinators to reproduce.

HOW EXACTLY DOES POLLINATION WORK?

Insects and animals transfer the pollen from the male to the female parts of a flower—from stamen to pistil—to allow for reproduction.

are being wiped out by a fungal disease called white-nose syndrome, which manifests as white fungus on their muzzles and wings.

OUR RESPONSIBILITY

Though the insects and pollinators may be declining today, there's a lot we can do to help them bounce back. Because of their vital role in pollination and in our ecosystems, butterflies, bats, and bees are all in need of our support and protection. They represent millions of other insects like beetles, wasps, thrips, and katydids that are also suffering significant declines in the wild. Sadly, these insects are floundering due primarily to human action and inaction. Major causes include excessive use of pesticides, increase in monoculture crops like corn and soybeans, urbanization, and habitat destruction.[9] In order to keep our crops and wildlife habitats functioning, we need to support the study of insect population trends and make changes to protect their future, our food supply, and the continued life of the planet's flowers, meadows, and more.

Pollination is critical to our survival. Approximately 85 percent of all plants—more than 150 food crops in the US—depend on pollinators to produce seed, which are key to forming the next generation of plants.[10] This, in turn, provides food for the next generation of pollinators and other life. Since the plants are rooted in place, pollinators act as the agent to transfer pollen for them.

A BIBLICAL PERSPECTIVE

God's character is revealed through nature. In Luke 12:27–28, Jesus said, "Consider how the wild flowers grow. They do not labor or spin. . . . That is how God clothes the grass of the field" (NIV). Have you thought about the fact that God uses the pollinators to grow the flowers and to "clothe" the grass of the field? In His creative and practical provision, God uses the insects to pollinate the flowers we love and to assist the crops we eat. Likewise, when it comes to giving us the things we need, God is practical, resourceful, and worthy of our trust.

A Lesson from Insects

The insects have something to teach us. Isaiah 40:22 says God "sits above the circle of the earth, and its inhabitants are like grasshoppers." Just as we are compared to flowers in Luke, here we are compared to grasshoppers—we're here for a short time and then gone, and our bodies return to the dust. Like grasshoppers, our lives are short and fleeting, while in contrast, God remains through all the ages.

How do we respond when faced with the reality of just how fleeting life is? If you're like me, you may be overwhelmed or frustrated by this thought, or you may try not to think about it at all! A healthy awareness of life's brevity teaches us "to number our days, that we may gain a heart of wisdom" (Psalm 90:12 NIV). This truth should remind each of us to live our lives connected to God and His eternal purposes that will outlast us. For whatever length of time we're here on this earth, we can be intentional and focused on doing God's work. Ephesians 2:10 tells us, "For we are God's handiwork, created in Christ Jesus to do good works, which God prepared in advance for us to do" (NIV). This good work includes our environmental care and actions.

The Resilience of Insects

Earth's bugs disappear by the billions. They're consumed by other animals, killed by changes in the weather, and easily stepped on without notice. Yet they are resilient in community and multiply at an astonishing rate. They quickly rebound from attack and destruction. Even though their lifespans can be as short as a few days, their jubilant noises and ceaseless activity persevere like praise.

When it comes to giving us the things we need, God is practical, resourceful, and worthy of our trust.

Paul explained what it was like for the apostles to live this way. "When reviled, we bless; when persecuted, we endure; when slandered, we entreat. We have become, and are still, like the scum of the world, the refuse of all things" (1 Corinthians 4:12–13). God's people are like this: when we are trampled on, threatened, cursed, and snuffed out, we rebound in exponential life and in the growth of new believers in God's family. And when facing the pressure of planetary stress, we can choose reactive love over indifferent passivity.

> **What would change in your life if you lived out your faith like a grasshopper?**

What would change in your life if you lived out your faith like a grasshopper? Knowing that you may not have tomorrow, how will you live with godly intentionality today? How will you treat others and this earth you've been given to care for in your limited time?

Incorporate Pollinator-Friendly Lawn-Care Practices

Some lawn-care methods inadvertently harm or kill pollinators. Stop harmful practices in your lawn and adopt beneficial practices to pollinator health.

CREATE A POLLINATOR-FRIENDLY MOWING SCHEDULE.

▸ Cut back on mowing by reducing to every two weeks. This has proven the best for bee populations, with 30 percent more bees visiting lawns mowed every other week than those mowed once a week.[11]

▸ The every-two-weeks mowing schedule provides local bees with foraging habitat through the growth of clover and dandelion. Let the clovers and dandelions bloom for a bit to help the bees, and then mow them down every other week.

ADD WILDERNESS CHARM.

▸ Add a wildflower meadow to your yard. It'll attract and support beautiful butterflies, bees, and birds.

▸ Grow edible plants in your yard that will attract pollinators and provide nutritious food for your home. Here are some to consider, depending on your location: squash, basil, green beans, lavender, apple trees, radishes, and sunflowers.

LEAVE DEBRIS.

▸ Piles of branches, dead leaves, and old trees make ideal homes for insects. Even small, hidden piles are a kindness!

Plant a Pollinator Garden

You can help save pollinators by making your yard more hospitable to them with a pollinator garden. If you do this with your church or neighborhood, it's a wonderful way to serve your community, plus you can organize volunteers to help with weeding and maintenance.

POLLINATOR GARDEN TIPS.

- Pollinator gardens require native plants for the best results. Your region will have specific conditions for specific plants. Insects (and other animals) in your area do much better with plants that grow naturally and have adapted in your region.

- The Xerces Society has a database for native pollinator plants for each region. You can also look up native plants on Audubon's database with your zip code.

- Choose a variety of plants that bloom from early spring into late fall. Include night-blooming flowers for bats and moths.

- Favor perennials because they grow back each year and require less maintenance.

- Designate a space with full or partial sunlight and use that nutrient-rich compost you made when you turned over the soil.

- Common pollinator plants that bees especially love (be sure to check if they are a good fit for your location): large-flowered collomia, bee balm, white heath aster, pink sparkler spirea, Mojave moss rose, penstemons or beardtongue, and coneflowers.

Build a Monarch Waystation

Monarchs migrate long distances and need stopover points, as well as habitats for feeding and laying eggs. Milkweed habitats are a game changer for monarchs to make a comeback. Make a waystation at your home, school, work, or church in a new space, or add to a current garden.

PLANT NATIVE MILKWEED.

- ▸ Monarch caterpillars are specialists, which means they eat *only* one kind of plant to turn into butterflies: milkweed. Choose and plant your local native varieties (plant at least two types).

PLANT NATIVE NECTAR FLOWERS.

- ▸ Monarchs require nectar from flowers for daily food, but especially for the energy needed to migrate from North America to overwintering grounds in Mexico.
- ▸ Start a new garden or add various nectar flowers to your current garden.

STRATEGICALLY SET UP YOUR BUTTERFLY STOPPING SPOT.

- ▸ Milkweed and nectar plants grow best in sunny areas in lighter soils (or with low clay content). Find an area where they will receive at least six hours of sun each day.
- ▸ Avoid plots with poor drainage to prevent root rot and allow for the soil to breathe.[12]

CERTIFY YOUR MONARCH WAYSTATION.

- ▸ Certify your monarch habitat through Monarch Watch online and receive a nifty sign to hang, plus a spot on the interactive map of other waystation neighbors.

Build or Buy a Bat Box

Provide for and support bats in your yard, and they will thank you by eating thousands of mosquitoes, while also pollinating at night. Plus, guano, or bat droppings, are an excellent natural fertilizer for gardens.

BAT BOX TIPS.

- ▸ You can provide a home for bats by building a bat box. Bat Conservation International's website provides free downloadable designs and instructions for two kinds: four-chamber and rocket boxes. They also have a map that shows what colors to paint your box depending on your region.

- ▸ Bat boxes can be purchased online as well. Buy a few and get friends together for crafting and decorate them with your own personal touch.

- ▸ Never disturb or touch a bat. They are generally not aggressive, but like other wildlife, they can carry disease. It's best to leave them alone to live their best bat lives, pollinating and hibernating.

- ▸ If bats are in your home, contact your local natural resource agency to have them humanely removed.

Limit or Stop Using Synthetic Pesticides and Herbicides

Pesticides are toxic to the environment (and some are known to cause cancer in humans). Look up Beyond Pesticides for specific guidance on how to control particular pests or weeds using alternatives to pesticides.

CREATIVE ALTERNATIVES.

- ▸ Nontoxic alternatives to pesticides include neem oil and diatomaceous earth (use carefully and sparingly because they can also kill beneficial insects).

- Natural predators like ladybugs for plants and nematodes for the soil (which feed on more than two hundred pests) are also helpful. Plant insectary plants (ones that attract helpful bugs) like mint, rosemary, thyme, and marigold.[13]

- To get rid of unwanted bugs, attract other insect-eating wildlife like birds by building a nesting box and adding bird feeders.

- Mulching is an eco-friendly way of preventing weeds, but check to make sure the mulch doesn't include herbicides.

Support and Volunteer with Conservation Organizations

CHECK OUT NONPROFITS THAT HELP POLLINATORS.

- Check out The Nature Conservancy, Bat Conservation International, and Xerces for ways to support pollinators.

GET INVOLVED IN A CITIZEN SCIENCE PROJECT.

- You can help count and monitor insect populations in your area and report your data to a project in the works. This is pretty cool, you citizen scientist you! Check out Xerces to get started.

CHAPTER EIGHT

WETLANDS

Nature's Beautiful Borders

> For this water goes there, that the waters of the sea may become fresh; so everything will live where the river goes.
>
> Ezekiel 47:9

HAVE YOU EVER NOTICED SWALLOWS DIVING AND INSECTS BUZZing in tall patches of grass in between shallow pools? If so, did you know you were likely by a wetland?

Wetlands are the buttresses bordering and protecting other ecosystems. They're the "transition zones" between land and water worlds. They provide vital services to every habitat they border or are a part of. Wetlands naturally filter and store harmful toxins and keep them from reaching our water systems and contaminating our water supply. They are also nature's way of preventing storm damage and absorbing water during floods. The roots of their plants strengthen the soil structure of the earth to combat erosion. Did you have any idea that wetlands were so uniquely significant?

Wetlands naturally filter and store harmful toxins and keep them from reaching our water systems and contaminating our water supply.

What Are Wetlands?

Wetlands are an area of land flooded or saturated with water seasonally or year-round. They contain plants adapted to watery conditions. The water can be salty, fresh, or somewhere in between, depending on where they're located. Wetlands by the coast are mostly salty and surround estuaries, which are partially enclosed bodies of water where rivers run into the sea, creating brackish (mix of fresh and salty) waters. Inland wetlands are usually fresh and located by lakes, ponds, and streams. They also occur in prairies and can spring up in areas where groundwater rises to the surface.

Many species rely on wetlands. Fish and shellfish use them for their nurseries, or habitat for their eggs, and for shelter and food. Migratory birds count on them for stopover points during their long journeys. In the continental US, wetlands take up only about 5 percent of the land area, but nearly half of all North American birds feed or nest in wetlands, while one-third of our endangered and threatened species depend on them.[1]

Wetlands also assist with preventing *harmful algal blooms* (HAB). HABs occur when bodies of water are overloaded with nutrients, which causes algae to grow rapidly, sucking out a lot of the oxygen in the water and resulting in massive fish kills (as mentioned previously). Some algal blooms are toxic to humans, known as *red tides* for the crimson color of blooms you can see from the shore and even from space. Wetlands work to absorb excess nutrients from fertilizer runoff and help prevent harmful algal blooms in rivers, lakes, and estuaries.

There are three main types of wetlands: swamps, marshes, and bogs. Swamps are like flooded forests with fluctuating water levels. Cypress, willows, and mangroves are common swamp trees. In the coastal tropics, mangroves' impressive root systems provide cage-like shelter for crabs, conchs, shrimp, and even seals. Marshes are dominated by grasses and shrubs and are loved by many birds, like the red-winged blackbird, great egret, and swarms of swallows, which find plenty of crabs and insects to feed on within the mud and vegetation. Bogs are found farther north in colder climates like Canada, Russia, and even the Arctic. They look like lakes filled with the collected debris of leaves, roots, and stems with moss and heather growing over the surface. Bogs are often home to gnarly carnivorous plants, like the pitcher plant and horned bladderwort, which lure, trap, and digest small invertebrates, but also grow pleasant things like cranberries.

Mangroves keep coastal zones healthy, providing habitat for thousands of species, stabilizing shorelines, preventing erosion, filtering pollution, including carbon dioxide, and protecting the land from waves and storms. They filter up to 90 percent of salt from seawater, and excrete it through glands and leaves, or through bark shedding. The destruction of mangroves in wetlands leads to coastal damage and increased flooding, along with the release of large amounts of carbon dioxide into the atmosphere.

The Mangrove Ecosystem

BACTERIA

GREAT BLUE HERON

WHITE IBIS

ALLIGATOR

BARNACLES

MANGROVE CRAB

GRASS SHRIMP

ORANGE SPONGE

PINFISH

COMMON SNOOK FISH

HERMIT CRAB

CUSHION SEA STAR

THE IMPORTANCE OF WETLANDS

Wetlands are the most underrated ecosystems on our planet, and they're disappearing three times faster than forests.[2] They're the habitat connectors, benefiting and supporting each ecosystem they touch. Between 1970 and 2015, about 35 percent of wetlands were lost globally, with the rate of destruction accelerating each year since 2000.[3] We've come a long way in understanding their importance and in taking steps to protect and restore them, but more needs to be done.

THE DISAPPEARANCE OF WETLANDS

We've lost more than half of our wetlands. They used to be seen as wastelands without much practical purpose. We filled them in to create farmlands, and we drained them and built cities—including San Francisco, Washington, DC, and St. Louis. Population increase and urbanization, especially of coastal areas and river deltas, drive wetland loss along with conversion to agricultural land. Today, wetlands are threatened by water drainage, pollution, invasive species, mismanaged dams, upstream erosion, and sediment dumping from deforestation.[4]

The coasts of the lower forty-eight states of the US lose eighty thousand acres of wetlands yearly. This is equivalent to around seven football fields of wetlands lost every hour.[5] A main driver of wetland loss on coasts is development, as nearly half of the

US population lives on the coasts. This loss threatens sustainable fisheries, endangered species, clean water supply, and shoreline protection from storms, floods, and tides. When we lose wetlands, coastal communities become more vulnerable to strong storms, like Hurricane Katrina in 2005, the costliest natural disaster in US history to date.

RESTORING AND BUILDING WETLANDS

Remember India's complex water problems from an earlier chapter—flooding during monsoons and wells running dry in droughts? Restoring and building wetlands is one helpful tactic for communities. Laying down concrete and other hard surfaces in development projects blocks rainwater from reaching the ground and exacerbates floods. Wetlands, on the other hand, absorb water and help to refill the groundwater in aquifers, storing up reserves during dry periods.

They're a nature-based solution to diverse environmental problems around the world spanning water scarcity, pollution, and endangered species.

As we've come to realize the subtle but powerful ways wetlands protect and provide for the rest of the planet and for us, we've put protections in place and begun restoring many areas. Ramsar is an international convention to safeguard the world's wetland habitats. It provides a framework for countries to conserve and wisely manage wetlands and their resources, but enforcement is often challenging.

It's crucial that we continue to protect and restore our wetlands. What's at stake? More intense flooding, storm damage, dangerous algal blooms, diminishing fish stocks, and toxins contaminating water sources! Wetlands also add a touch of nature's beauty and serenity amid busy urban and suburban lives, with recreational activities like kayaking, fishing, and bird watching. They should increasingly become a prized part of our cities, neighborhoods, and public lands. They're a nature-based solution to diverse environmental problems around the world spanning water scarcity, pollution, and endangered species.

OUR RESPONSIBILITY

We can combine technology-based and nature-based approaches to find the most appropriate, beneficial ways of coexisting and connecting with our natural areas. Instead of manufacturing ecologically harsh structures like concrete seawalls on the coasts to protect properties, wetlands naturally lessen storm damage and help prevent floods. When we incorporate wetland habitats and other natural elements to guard our coasts, we're developing what's known as "living shorelines," a growing nature-based strategy around our waterways.

There's something sacred about the human desire to save the planet.

There's something sacred about the human desire to save the planet. A refusal to succumb to apathy toward the diverse plights of our world is honorable and resembles the enduring hope of heaven for ultimate restoration. But we'd do well to make sure our striving isn't only in our own efforts and that we aren't placing our trust in human ingenuity and technological advances alone (although these are an important part of environmental solutions). The desire to save the world comes from the heart of God, and He wants to partner with us in our efforts to fix what's broken. If we start with a wisdom like we see in the wetlands, we will prioritize ways of sustaining and upholding community health around us, for both humans and wildlife.

A BIBLICAL PERSPECTIVE

Does Scripture provide insight into how we should take care of and manage our wetlands? Like many other practical decisions in our lives, including environmental choices, the Bible points us to the value of wisdom in handling complex issues. How we steward the land and resources requires discerning the best options for each unique time, place, and circumstance.

God's Wise Design

Wetlands aren't necessarily the first topic you think of for earth care, but in His wisdom, God often uses things the world overlooks

> **God is always working wonders through His creation and through our circumstances.**

as insignificant and small—think fishermen disciples—for His grand design. Psalm 104:24 speaks about the role of wisdom in the formation of the natural world: "O LORD, how manifold are your works! In wisdom you have made them all." God founded the earth by and through wisdom (Proverbs 3:19).

God created wetland ecosystems to absorb the toxins and salt and to produce and sustain life. How unexpected, and how good! As Christians, we shouldn't be surprised that God uses the places that seem useless, because as you may have noticed, God is always working wonders through His creation and through our circumstances. It's in God's character to use the unexpected places to work out His plan. And lo and behold, as we've just learned, these often-unnoticed places are literally protecting and providing for you and me, even when we don't notice it.

Nature's Wisdom in Harmony

As we look for wisdom to solve environmental challenges, we should strive for solutions that bring peace, connection, and communal flourishing. This kind of wisdom looks at different options from multiple sides and points of view and finds solutions that benefit each part or person involved.

For example, we know a city has a need for housing and business development, but people also have needs for clean air and water and land that can support heavy rainfall and provide a source of water during heat waves. Wise planning includes an awareness of all these needs and seeks to build the city in a way that also helps the land to thrive and provide. Vancouver, Canada, built and grew a wetland in the middle of the city near a stream (where it's home to the city's beaver resident, Justin Beaver!). Wetlands are a nature-based, long-lasting solution to many environmental problems for our cities, coasts, grasslands, and forests.

We often look to and rely on technology and human inventions to solve our problems, which isn't necessarily wrong. But as Christians, we should feel confident in the inherent design of nature to be a wise guide for developing environmental solutions. Often, nature's solutions aren't outwardly impressive but moderate in approach. Our stack of impressive, ever-progressing technologies can reach Tower-of-Babel levels, but our efforts should first aim to understand God's design (like the functioning of wetlands) and cooperate with His ingenuity in the natural workings of nature.

Get to Know the Wetlands in Your Area

Wetlands are surprisingly ubiquitous! They're present on the coasts, in parks, and even highway medians and low-lying areas in cities, towns, and forests. You may be near some of the bigger landmarks with wetlands like the Great Lakes, Gulf of Mexico, Long Island Sound, Chesapeake Bay, or San Francisco Bay.

EXPLORE YOUR LOCAL WETLANDS.

- ▸ Look into your local parks or contact your parks and recreation department to find out where the wetlands are near you. Put on some boots you don't mind getting dirty and go check them out!

- ▸ Find a field guide and educate yourself on the intricacies and wonders of wetland habitats. Learn how they benefit the systems around them through their fauna and flora.

- ▸ Wetlands have zones of various plant types suited to the specific conditions of dampness and salt levels, like upland vegetation, fringing (or bordering) vegetation, and aquatic vegetation where the water table is higher.

ADVOCATE FOR WETLAND PROTECTIONS IN YOUR AREA.

- ▸ Federal, state, and local governments each have structured responsibilities in enforcing rules and regulations affecting wetlands. Federal and state involvement comes through the Clean Water Act. Local city and county governments typically enforce zoning and development restrictions.

- ▸ The conversion of farmland to development property has been responsible for the steady decline of wetland acreage in the US. Understand and oppose such projects by advocating for stronger protections in community planning and zoning regulations.

▸ Support enhanced open space requirements, removal of invasive species, floodplain development prohibitions, and Low Impact Development (LID) strategies around wetlands.

Use Mindful Lawn Practices to Support Wetland Health

Our lawns are part of the larger watersheds of our area, which drain into nearby streams and wetlands when it rains. Therefore, what we do on our properties matters for wetland health and protection. Rain gardens and pocket wetlands in yards slow the water flow and allow the ground to absorb and plants to naturally treat the water before it reaches streams and wetlands.

PLANT A RAIN GARDEN.

▸ When it rains, water collects and flows from your roof, driveway, and other hard surfaces. A rain garden catches the runoff, allowing it to soak into the ground and filter out pollutants.

▸ A rain garden is a garden of native shrubs, perennials, and flowers planted in a depressed area of a landscape.

▸ Plant native vegetation in your rain garden considering extent of sun exposure, ability to absorb rainwater, ability to uptake nutrients, and resistance to drought. Have fun and choose which plants speak to your taste in yard design.

BUILD A BROAD-CRESTED SWALE.

▸ A broad-crested swale is a wide and shallow depression that creates a path to direct water. A swale collects runoff from driveways and roofs and channels the water into a rain garden.

▸ You can build the depression with a shovel or rent an excavator. Many people choose to fill the swale with a layer of rocks, which slows the water and looks nice, like a rock path.

CONSIDER A POCKET WETLAND.

- Depending upon the amount of runoff, the number of discharge points, and elevation changes, the swale may extend to a larger area where you can construct a pocket wetland.

- A pocket wetland should be built to detain or retain water seasonally. Native wetland plants should be planted specifically to uptake nutrients from yard fertilizer and chemicals from driveway and parking lot runoff.

- The work is worth it when you have waterfowl and other charming wildlife visiting your yard, plus it's great for the local environment.

RESIST PESTICIDE, FERTILIZER, AND HERBICIDE USE.

- Avoid pesticide and fertilizer use if at all possible or use very sparingly (see chapter 7 for possible alternatives).

- If you struggle with pests, try using natural products, such as soap or plant-based insecticides. For fertilizer, you can make mulch out of lawn clippings and leaves.

- Refrain from adding fertilizers or pesticides to your lawn before it rains because the rain will easily wash it away.

Consider Conservation Easements for Your Property

In the US, around three-fourths of the remaining wetlands are on private lands.[6] State and local natural resource agencies and environmental nonprofits, like The Nature Conservancy, work with individual landowners to set up conservation easements and management actions to protect and steward wetlands on private property.

THE AGRICULTURAL CONSERVATION EASEMENT PROGRAM (ACEP)

- The ACEP helps landowners, land trusts, indigenous tribes, and local governments work together to protect, restore, and enhance wetlands and other landscapes through conservation easements.

- Landowners hold the greatest potential for restoring and protecting our wetlands. If this applies to you and you want to make a difference, you don't have to figure it out alone.

- NRCS, part of USDA, provides private property owners with technical and financial assistance for restoring and maintaining wetlands.

- NRCS prioritizes applications with potential for improving habitat for migratory birds and other wildlife. They develop and put into practice a wetland reserve restoration easement plan to restore and enhance wetlands for each property.

- To enroll land through wetland reserve easements, landowners are invited to apply at any time at their local USDA Service Center.

- Ducks Unlimited (DU) also has decades of experience working with landowners to secure wetland conservation easements on their property to protect them from future development. Check out DU's Conservation Easement Program if you think your property may be a fit!

Support Nonprofits Working to Protect and Restore Wetlands

Get involved with a nonprofit working with wetlands or gather a church group to connect with and support local wetland restoration efforts.

- **Ducks Unlimited** focuses on wetland protection and restoration across the US and Canada.

- Visit the **Environmental Protection Agency (EPA)** website for examples of state and local wetland monitoring programs. Go to epa.gov/wetlands for resources and contacts. Also look into EPA regional contacts, US Army Corps of Engineers (USACE) contacts, and Association of State Wetland Managers to get involved in wetland projects near you.

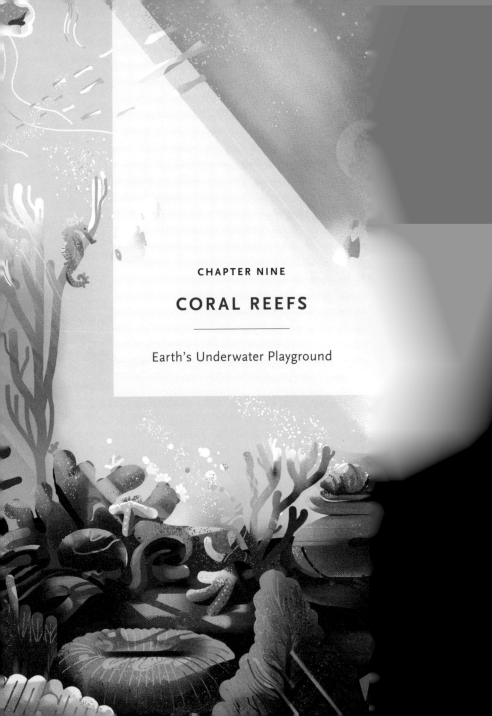

CHAPTER NINE

CORAL REEFS

Earth's Underwater Playground

In his teaching the islands will put their hope.

ISAIAH 42:4 NIV

WHEN SUNRAYS STRIKE THE BRANCHES AND PLATES OF CORAL reefs, colors flash and flicker as sea life—clownfish, starfish, sea-horses, and anemones—dance and sway in these underwater realms. Although coral reefs take up less than 1 percent of the ocean's area, nearly 25 percent of all marine creatures rely on them.[1] Their biodiversity is so great, they're dubbed the "rainforest of the sea." Yet largely due to human actions, they're in grave trouble. If we don't make changes now, we could lose 90 percent of our coral reefs,[2] both their nautical wonders and their practical provisions.

THE DESTRUCTION OF CORAL

While some of the coral reef destruction is due to natural occurrences, unfortunately much of the damage has been caused by human carelessness. By becoming educated and more intentional about our human activity, we can stop some of the damage being done to this magnificent part of God's creation.

Warming Waters

From 2014 to 2017, unusually warm waters impacted 70 percent of coral reefs around the world in a massive coral bleaching event.[3] Australia's Great Barrier Reef saw hundreds of miles of corals turn from vibrant colors to chalky white. Mass mortality of half of Australia's Great Barrier Reef followed the warming events of 2016 and 2017, and it may never fully recover.[4]

Coral bleaching occurs when the corals are stressed by changes in external conditions, like warming waters, and react by expelling algae that live inside them. The algae provide the corals with their food and their color, so when they eject them, the corals turn white and become deathly ill. Humans play a major part in the warmer waters causing this harm with our greenhouse gas emissions.[5] While corals can recover from bleaching, they need cooler water and steady conditions to recuperate, which can take decades.

What Is Coral?

Corals are animals. Their soft bodies have rotund bases with tentacles (each one is called a polyp) extending up into the water. They may look like plants attached to rocks and hard surfaces, but the coral polyps move, expanding and contracting in the water. These animals construct the giant sea architecture of the reefs. The corals build layer upon layer of the limestone reefs, which become habitat for fish, urchins, sponges, sharks, rays, lobster, octopus, snails, and more.

Overfishing, Pollution, and Buildup

In addition to warming ocean waters, other threats to coral reefs make this recovery difficult. Overfishing and other destructive human practices around the reefs diminish our fish supply, which can be disastrous for the reefs. In a healthy coral reef ecosystem, fish feed on the algae. Without them, the algae build up around the coral, ultimately suffocating them and blocking the sunlight, leading to the reefs' demise. The pollution we contribute from things like plastic, industrial runoff, sewage, and oil is also poisoning reefs. And when dirt from human construction, logging, and mining reaches the ocean from beaches and rivers, the reefs become smothered by sediment buildup.

Pollution, sediments, toxins, chemicals, and excessive nutrients reach the coasts by traveling downstream through watersheds into streams and rivers flowing into the ocean. This disrupts coastal habitats, including tide pools, and it's especially detrimental to coral reefs. With coral bleaching, acidification, and disease, corals need pollution-free water if they're going to have a chance at survival.

$\rightarrow$

The coral reef structure is made of thousands of polyps. This illustration shows the basic anatomy of a single polyp—the main part of the structure affected by coral bleaching. Bleaching occurs when corals expel algae that live inside their tissue, causing them to fade, often turning completely white. When the ocean gets too warm, the coral becomes stressed and expels the vital algae.

Anatomy *of a* Coral

MOUTH

POLYPS

TENTACLES

GUT
CAVITY

TISSUE
CONNECTION
BETWEEN POLYPS

MESENTERIAL
FILAMENTS

BARE SKELETON
OF POLYP

> **God built His creation to work holistically.**

Human activity is also causing our oceans to become more acidic at an alarming rate. Simple daily activities like driving your car or using electricity emit carbon dioxide into the air, which is then absorbed into the ocean. This makes it challenging for corals to build their reefs, and if the water reaches a certain level of acidity, the reefs can literally begin to dissolve. All these issues compound on one another and make it difficult for corals to recover from bleaching and also makes them more vulnerable to deadly diseases.

THE IMPORTANCE OF CORAL

Corals are more than admirable architects of the marine realm; they are indispensable to us and to the planet. In addition to providing opportunities for recreational activities like snorkeling, they protect coasts from storm damage and support the local economy. We also count on them as a food source, and we've discovered medicinal products in their ecosystems. More than half a billion people rely on coral reefs for food, income, and protection. If putting a price on it is helpful for grasping the magnitude of coral reef benefits, the net economic value of the world's coral reefs is estimated to be nearly tens of billions of US dollars per year.[6] We also must consider their inherent, priceless worth as our oceans' natural treasures.

A BIBLICAL PERSPECTIVE

God built His creation to work holistically, and when everything is in balance, the results can be absolutely dazzling. You see, the corals are made up of multiple species living closely together in harmony. The algae and coral need each other for nutrition and protection— they can't survive without one another.

Symbiotic Ecosystem

This symbiotic relationship between microbe and fauna also gives the corals their signature bright colors. God saw that *it was good* to meet the practical needs of coral reefs in a way that makes them captivating. He provides for His creation and makes it beautiful all at once.

How can this underwater symbiotic design teach us to interact with nature? Well, given that about 40 percent of the world's population live near our coasts, we Christians need to champion the symbiosis that God designed for these ecosystems. We work, play, learn, fish, eat, and live our lives right by these amazing coastal habitats and share the space daily. We must acknowledge that we are *in relationship* with these reefs, and we have been blessed with an opportunity to preserve them. Coral reefs are God's underwater gardens and a legacy of His creative work, which we're called to look after.

One of the hesitancies Christians have in engaging with and enjoying the natural world is the fear of worshiping nature rather

> **When our appreciation for nature's beauty is linked to our gratitude toward its provision through and connection to Christ, we can confidently enjoy creation, including the magnificent coral reefs, and give God glory.**

than the Creator. To sharpen our discernment on this topic, it's helpful to contrast the Christian mentality with what it's not—pantheism. In its simplistic definition, *pantheism* is the belief that God *is* everything. There is no distinction made between God and the universe.

The key distinction for Christian creation theology is that it upholds God's *transcendence* and *immanence*. In other words, no matter how mysteriously close (immanent) His Spirit is with living beings and all of nature, He is ultimately separate (transcendent) from it in essence. God became part of the physical fabric of the universe, and "put on matter," when He became incarnate in Jesus. When our appreciation for nature's beauty is linked to our gratitude toward its provision through and connection to Christ, we can confidently enjoy creation, including the magnificent coral reefs, and give God glory.

Trusting God

As caretakers of nature, we should be careful taking from it excessively. Pursuing money and idolizing wealth and prosperity is a sin issue in our hearts, and the irony is that when we carelessly overfish our reefs or opt for modes of transportation that emit carbon dioxide, we also harm ourselves in the long run.

Greedy actions like these often stem from our fear that we will not have enough or be provided for. But as we can see from God's design in nature, He will provide for us. That's who He is. He is a provider. Look at the reefs. The corals absorb tiny algae with their tentacles, the seahorses find homes in the crannies and nooks of the reefs, and the clownfish find refuge in the anemones. Every unique creature is considered and provided for by God's evolutionary design in coral reefs, and the result is *beautiful*. How much more will the Father take care of us and give us the good things we need (Matthew 7:11)? We can rest knowing that God provides for His creation, and this comfort can stir us to be generous toward nature, particularly the reefs.

Mindfully Visit Tourist Spots as a Gracious, Green Guest

KEEP THESE RECREATION AND TOURISM TIPS IN MIND.

Coastal and marine tourism supports more than 6.5 million jobs.[7]
However, tourism and increasing coastal development can also be a
source of harm to coastal environments. Be aware of your actions as a
tourist when you travel, and leave the area better than you found it.

RECREATION AND TOURISM TIPS.

- If you dive or snorkel, don't touch or disrupt corals. Stirring up
  sediment can smother corals. Admire only!

- Don't purchase coral products as souvenirs. Find a cool shark
  figurine, snazzy airbrushed T-shirt, or literally anything else not taken
  from the sea.

- Avoid dropping your boat anchor or chain near a coral reef; look for
  a sandy bottom or use available moorings.

- Chemicals in sunscreen can accumulate in coral tissues and cause
  bleaching, damage, deformation, and even death. Protect your skin
  and protect coral—buy only marine-friendly sunscreen. Check out
  the National Oceanic and Atmospheric Administration's (NOAA)
  sunscreen webpage for more information.

LEARN ABOUT SUSTAINABLE COASTAL DEVELOPMENT.

- Building new homes, businesses, resorts, and hotels on the coast
  requires dredging and intense construction on beaches. Dirt and
  debris can pile up in the ocean and block coral from sunlight,
  causing bleaching and death.

- Coastal development projects are a huge undertaking, and there are regulations and policies that need to be put in place and/or better enforced. Advocacy opportunities are important for coastal communities to stand up for their coastal areas.

▸ If you don't live near a coast, when you visit as a tourist, look into the resort or place you are choosing to stay. Sewage dumping from tourist complexes is a major issue. The sewage smothers coral, causes algal overgrowth, and can prevent corals from recovering after bleaching events.[8] Inquire into the waste management practices of your tourist destination.

Be Responsible for the Reefs, No Matter Your Location

KEEP YOUR PROPERTY WATERSHED-FRIENDLY.

▸ Whether you are landlocked or live on the coast, cleaning up your local watershed can ultimately affect bodies of water and habitats downstream.

▸ Avoid sending chemicals into our waterways by eliminating or significantly reducing use of fertilizers, pesticides, and herbicides.

▸ Pick up litter in a neighborhood or city area with a church group; especially target trash near stormwater drains.

VOLUNTEER AT BEACH CLEANUPS.

▸ Whether you live near the coast or plan on visiting a beach in the future, you can get involved in beach or reef cleanups (best excuse to visit the beach!).

▸ Visit the websites for the Ocean Conservancy, Surfrider Foundation, Ocean Blue Project, or a local coastal organization to learn about opportunities to help.

▸ If you plan on visiting the Florida Keys in particular, bear in mind that reef systems off the coast are struggling with coral disease outbreaks and are extra sensitive to any form of pollution.

Choose Sustainable Seafood

Make sure the seafood you consume comes from a fishery that's not contributing to crashing fish populations. Fish are an important part of the coastal food web, and they also help keep algae in check that could otherwise outcompete and smother coral.

MAKE INFORMED SEAFOOD PURCHASES TO HELP PREVENT OVERFISHING.

▸ We don't have to give up seafood altogether, but we do need to make sure our seafood is sustainably sourced to prevent overfishing.

▸ Look for various certification labels including the Marine Stewardship Council (MSC), Aquaculture Stewardship Council (ASC), Global Seafood Alliance, Best Aquaculture Practices (BAP), Friend of the Sea, and Naturland.

FAVOR LOCALLY CAUGHT SEAFOOD.

▸ Join a community-supported fishery (CSF) and help support local fishermen and promote sustainable practices. Visit localcatch.org to find a CSF near you.

▸ If a CSF isn't an option for you, be inquisitive and choosy about your seafood purchases. Ask retailers and restaurants about their fishing sources.

CHECK OUT SUSTAINABLE SEAFOOD GUIDES AND APPS.

▸ Some helpful guides include Monterey Bay Aquarium's Seafood Watch, Ocean Wise, FishWatch, and WWF seafood guides on its website and iPhone app.

Support Nonprofits

THESE NONPROFITS ARE WORKING TO ESTABLISH MARINE PROTECTED
AREAS AND SAVE CORAL REEFS:

- ▶ **Mission Blue** works to set up marine protected areas (MPA) that protect coral reefs and other valuable marine life from fishing and other potentially harmful human activities. Similar to national parks, it keeps coastal areas in pristine condition.

- ▶ **Coral Reef Alliance**'s mission is to save coral reefs around the world. It works with coastal communities to lessen threats to reefs, like dealing with sewage and waste management issues, and it researches how reefs adapt to climate change to inform solutions.

- ▶ **The Nature Conservancy** is an organization on the forefront of living shoreline development to help coastal communities prepare for sea level rise and intense storms, among many other things. There may also be local environmental organizations in your area working to promote living shoreline solutions, like Save the Sound in Connecticut and New York.

CHAPTER TEN

THE OCEAN

Our Immense and
Unsearchable Waters

Who spread out the earth upon the waters, His love endures forever.
PSALM 136:6 (NIV)

WHEN YOU THINK ABOUT THE OCEAN, DO YOU PICTURE WAVES
crashing on the sand, endless shades of blues and greens swirling to
the horizon, or whales below and seabirds above? Though most of
us have idyllic perceptions of our planet's largest bodies of water,
the oceans suffer because of human activity and careless choices.

What Is the Ocean?

The ocean is one connected, colossal body of salt water covering
more than 70 percent of the surface of planet Earth. We divide it
up geographically into four regions: the Pacific, Atlantic, Indian,
and Arctic oceans. Around 97 percent of the world's water fills the
ocean basins. This volume moves and churns within and between
each region through currents and gyres, which are large systems of
circulating ocean currents that move either clockwise or counter-
clockwise around the ocean basins. These massive forces mix the
ocean and influence its biology down to the tiniest marine critters,
the plankton.

The oceans are home to abundant sea life. They've been crucial to travel and industry. And they transport nutrients and regulate the climate. But they also carry our litter, forming slowly spinning whirlpools of trash called *garbage patches*. The pollution we've made is disrupting and destroying life at every level.

THE PROBLEMS AFFECTING OUR OCEANS

We have several challenges facing us as we look at the problems affecting our oceans. We'll look at how to take this from a global view down to the individual perspective.

Pollution

Pollution in our oceans is a huge problem. After production, 79 percent of plastic is "thrown away" in the trash (often after only one use) and taken to a landfill,[1] or "thrown away" into nature. Without change and action, by 2050 there could be a pound of plastic for every three pounds of fish in the ocean.[2] It's estimated that greater than eight million metric tonnes, roughly the weight of eighty million blue whales,[3] of plastic enter our ocean every year, contributing to the ocean's "garbage patches," or a "trash soup" of sorts, with litter floating around and polluting the water column.

> **The pollution we've made is disrupting and destroying life at every level.**

The largest example of trash accumulating in the ocean is the Great Pacific Garbage Patch, which floats between Hawaii and California. There are also congregations of marine debris, mostly plastics, circulating in all five gyres. Plastic trash that washes into rivers, lakes, and oceans harms marine and freshwater environments in numerous ways.

Microplastics

The majority of the plastic pieces, called *microplastics*, have been broken down and are very small. Microplastics are a major issue because fish, waterfowl, and other sea creatures consume them. For example, albatrosses are giant seabirds that look like a mix between a seagull and pelican. They skim the ocean surface with their beaks to scoop up food, but instead they often pick up plastic. On Midway Atoll, a group of Hawaiian Islands, decaying albatrosses were found with abdomens full of shards of plastic and bottle caps. It's a sad shock—their stomachs become trash bags for our litter.

Plastic has been discovered in 59 percent of seabirds,[4] in all sea turtle species,[5] and in more than 25 percent of the fish in world sea markets.[6] The

> It's estimated that greater than eight million metric tonnes, roughly the weight of eighty million blue whales, of plastic enter our ocean every year, contributing to the ocean's "garbage patches," or a "trash soup" of sorts, with litter floating around and polluting the water column.

smaller particles are also known to absorb toxins from the environment, which when ingested by sea creatures, may accumulate in their systems and transfer up the food chain all the way to humans. Plastic litter can come back to us in this unfortunate way and poorly affect our health in carcinogenic and pathological ways we are still learning about.

Ocean Acidification (Carbon Pollution)

Another type of pollution that's negatively affecting our oceans is carbon pollution. A problem called *ocean acidification* occurs when there is excess carbon dioxide (from vehicles and industrial plants) in the atmosphere that is naturally absorbed by the ocean waters. Oceans absorb around 30 percent of the CO_2 released into the air.[7] This increases the acidity of the water and affects the wildlife of the sea. Many marine species are used to surviving at specific acidity levels, and fluctuations can be detrimental.

This is especially true for species that rely on calcium carbonate (which dissolves under more acidic conditions) for their shells and homes. We've already discussed one animal this impacts—corals. Ocean acidification is also bad news for the shellfish we use as a productive food source. Finally, certain types of plankton—tiny free-floating organisms that make up the base of the ocean's food web—are especially vulnerable to the acidifying waters. This can in turn impact populations of fish that prey on them and then the bigger sea creatures, like dolphins and seals, which count on these fish for food.

Overfishing

Another challenge for our oceans is overfishing, which happens when we take more fish out of the ocean than is naturally able to rebound. Fish stocks crash when we don't let the fish populations build back up. The exact number is often debated by conservation scientists, but the UN estimates that about a third of global fisheries are overharvested.[8] This practice threatens not only the fisheries and people who depend on them to make a living, but it also threatens our food security and the protein supply billions of people depend on around the world. Fishing itself isn't wrong, but it's unwise and shortsighted to deplete the resource rapidly. We're stealing from our futures. In certain areas, like the US coasts, there have recently been encouraging signs that some fisheries are on the path to recovery thanks to sustainable fishing enforcement, and we can help this trend continue by purchasing sustainable seafood.

THE IMPORTANCE OF THE OCEAN

It's difficult to overstate how instrumental oceans are to the health of our entire planet. The oceans help to regulate the climate by transmitting heat from the equator to the poles. We count on oceans for around half of the oxygen produced on earth; most of this comes from tiny photosynthesizing plankton (they're amazing!).[9] Kelp forests and seagrass beds capture carbon dioxide and are a vital part of climate change solutions. What's known as marine protected areas

(MPA) is one key conservation tactic with regulations like no-fishing zones to help protect ocean habitats (like coral reefs and kelp forests) and allow areas to bounce

We're stealing from our futures.

back. Billions of people rely on fish from the ocean for their main source of protein. The ocean affects our weather, breathing, and food. Plus, it's an unending source of exploration, recreation, and wonder.

A BIBLICAL PERSPECTIVE

If you've ever sat on a beach and watched the sun rise over the great expanse of the ocean, then you've likely experienced how an earthly view can inspire feelings of heavenly wonder in us. The water glimmers at the light of dawn as the sky is streaked in oranges and pinks above what appears to be an endless horizon. The ocean's immensity and unsearchable depths put us in awe and help us know God and His love better.

Our Duty to Others and the Earth

Many people deliberately litter or dump their trash on the ground, on this sacred earth upheld by a holy God. We have the opportunity to graciously pick up the mess of others out of love for God and respect for His handiwork. By cleaning up after others, we serve them in a way they may never know about or appreciate,

Microplastics *in the* Ocean

INDUSTRY & POWER PLANTS

Source of pollutants

UV

Fisheries

BIOACCUMULATION

Human food source

Macroplastic

Contaminants & Toxins

ADSORPTION

Secondary consumer

Microplastic

but this gives us an opportunity to love others and the earth selflessly.

Jesus is Lord over the sea and its winds and waves.

Even more than litter or mess, perhaps the greater harm is due to our negligence. It's easy to think our own waste vanishes when we throw it in the bin, but it builds up in trash piles, escapes into waterways, and often lands in the ocean. The garbage patches of the ocean reveal the negligence of our excess waste and plastic pollution problem. As Christians, we should mitigate our waste and find solutions to clean and beautify the earth for God's glory.

The Remarkable Ocean

Like all parts of nature, the ocean is under God's design and command. He created the ocean to be moved and stirred by the forces of the sun, moon, air pressure, and wind. The periodic, or seasonal, arrangement of the earth, moon, and sun animates the wind and changes the air pressure all around our planet, oscillating the tides, churning up the currents, and revolving the ocean basins into gyres.

Microplastics—pieces smaller than 5 mm in size—are present in the oceans around the world. They're formed when larger pieces of plastic are broken down by waves, wind, and UV radiation from the sun. Through adsorption, contaminants and toxins bind to microplastics. Ingestion of these microplastics moves the chemicals up the food chain from plankton, to small fish, to larger fish and mammals, and then to humans—a process called bioaccumulation.

God spoke these mechanisms in motion, whether by a flare of light at the Big Bang or another cosmic phenomenon, which put the sun and moon in their places. The cycles of the moon are dictated by His foreseen guidance. The earth's tilt is divinely determined. Like a skilled mathematician with a protractor and compass, God "drew" the earth's orbit around the sun. All these titanic forces combine to form the winds and the waves.

> As humans encroach upon and explore every corner of the planet, we need to do so with kindness, awe, and wonder.

It's so utterly remarkable that during His time on earth, Jesus held the wind and waves at His command. Only a God-man could do that. Matthew 8:27 exclaims, "What sort of man is this, that even winds and sea obey him?" When Jesus stilled the storm, it led the disciples to recognize Him as the Christ. We, too, can see His power and authority in the magnitude and mystery of the ocean. Jesus is Lord over the sea and its winds and waves.

The Mysterious Ocean

Though it's getting a lot of attention with science research, global warming warnings, new expeditions, territorial disputes, and international debate, the ocean is still widely unexplored. We still have more than 80 percent of the ocean to explore and map.[10] People talk about space as the last frontier, but we have many mysteries to discover and unfold about the great blue water basins right here on our own planet.

As it says in Psalm 104:25: "Here is the sea, great and wide, which teems with creatures innumerable, living things both small and great." The depths of the underworld in the Atlantic, Pacific, and Indian oceans are suspenseful settings of deep darkness and hidden creatures: giant squids, glowing fish, bizarre and enormous marine mammals. It's the frightening sublime. The mystery of the ocean draws us and beckons us to explore.

As humans encroach upon and explore every corner of the planet, we need to do so with kindness, awe, and wonder. God invites us to learn more about the works of His hands, but never just for our own ends or by means that are harmful. As Christians, we need to lead with God-sized wisdom to know what explorations to fund and how best to steward and care for the ocean.

Follow the Four *R*s: Refuse, Reduce, Reuse, Recycle

It's estimated that 17.6 billion pounds of plastic make it from the land and into our oceans every year. This is like dumping a garbage truck full of plastic into our oceans each minute.[11] Every person has a role to play in preventing more trash from entering the ocean, and it starts with our daily habits.

REFUSE SINGLE-USE PLASTIC.

- ▸ Eliminate your use of single-use plastics like straws, plastic cutlery, paper coffee cups, plastic water bottles, and plastic bags. Single-use is senseless waste! Marine wildlife can get caught in the straps of plastic bags and sea turtles often mistake floating plastic bags for jellyfish and try to eat them.

- ▸ Buy a travel-size carrying pack of reusable utensils. REI has some nifty packs you can carry with you, or you can find options online.

- ▸ Ditch plastic straws. Straws can choke and impale the soft tissue of marine animals. Keep a reusable straw handy if needed. Or be extreme and just sip from your cup!

- ▸ Bring your favorite travel coffee cup with you to coffee shops, or become a coffee expert and connoisseur at home.

- ▸ If you use a Keurig or similar coffee maker, use a reusable coffee filter pod with freshly ground coffee instead of plastic K-Cups.

- ▸ Food packaging is one of the most common forms of litter found during the Ocean Conservancy's cleanups.[12] Bring your own reusable produce bags to the grocery or farmers markets, and avoid food prewrapped in plastic.

- ▸ Replace plastic cling wrap with reusable wax wraps, like Bee's Wrap. They have an array of fun and lovely patterns to choose from.

- Bring your own takeout containers to restaurants, or order only as much as you can eat. Instead of plastic bags for snacks and sandwiches, buy reusable snack packs like Stasher silicone reusable food storage bags.

- Keep reusable shopping bags in your car or in a noticeable place at home to always remember to bring them with you when you shop.

- Minimize your online orders or select options to combine packages when possible.

- Buy in bulk more often to reduce the amount of food packaging, which should save you money as well.

- Use microfiber-catching laundry balls, bags, or filters.

REUSE AND RECYCLE.

- Host clothing swaps or yard sales with your friends or with your community. Your "trash" may be a new treasure for a friend!

- Learn your area's recycling rules and continue to check your community's recycling list, as it can change. Recycle everything you can't reduce or refuse if it's on the list above.

REDUCE.

- When you can't refuse, reuse, or recycle, at least try to reduce wherever you can.

Use Plastic Alternatives

As we refuse, reuse, reduce, and recycle, we also need to shift production of materials toward alternatives to plastic, which remain on the planet for hundreds of years. Other options are being developed and improved that are biodegradable and more eco-friendly in their production process.

CLEANING PRODUCTS

- Cleaning products are made up of mostly water. Try Blueland supplies reusable bottles and dissolvable tablets.

SHAMPOO AND CONDITIONER BARS

- To reduce plastic from our beauty and skincare products, try shampoo, conditioner, and bodywash bars by brands like by Humankind, Chagrin Valley Soap, or other brands to find one that works well for you.

MICROFIBER-FREE DISH CLOTHS

- Choose bamboo-fiber cloths over microfiber cloths or disposable paper towels. They are safe to wash and come from abundant and fast-growing bamboo plants. Check out Whiff Botanicals/Whiffkitch bamboo dish cloths and kitchen wipes.

COMPOSTABLE KITCHEN SPONGES

- Buy dye-free compostable sponges like Sqwishful sponges, which are made from plant-based cellulose.

SHOES MADE FROM RECYCLED PLASTIC

- Rothy's is an innovative shoe brand that makes machine washable shoes made from recycled materials like water bottles and marine plastic.

Lead or Join Ocean Cleanups

Cleaning up the great garbage patches in our ocean's gyres seems insurmountable, but there are mega projects underway to attempt to clean it, like the Dutch floating trash collector with a nearly two-thousand-foot boom that was sent into the Pacific Garbage Patch from

San Francisco. The best, most cost-effective thing individuals can do right now is prevent any more plastic trash from entering the marine environment.

COASTAL CLEANUPS

- Litter on our streets and beaches and in our rivers and streams can become marine debris. Subscribe online to NOAA's monthly newsletter to receive updates on cleanups that may be happening near you.

- When you visit a beach, bring a recycled trash bag with you to pick up litter and leave the area better than when you found it.

- Challenge yourself to aim for zero waste. Start by eliminating a few items at a time and work up to it. Check out zero-waste guides online and Instagram handles with endless creative zero-waste tips.

Support Ocean Nonprofits and International Programs

LOOK INTO THESE ORGANIZATIONS TO SEE HOW YOU CAN HELP.

- **Oceana** is focused entirely on ocean conservation. It works to create MPAs, it's already safeguarded more than four million square miles of ocean, and it works to protect endangered marine species like the North Atlantic right whale.

- **Ocean Conservancy** is an advocacy group dedicated to protecting marine habitats, promoting sustainable fisheries, and reducing human impacts on the ocean. It also leads annual international beach cleanups.

CHAPTER ELEVEN

THE POLES AND GLOBAL CLIMATE

Our Planet's Future

From whose womb did the ice come forth, and
who has given birth to the frost of heaven?

JOB 38:29

THE SNOWY POLES OF OUR EARTH DEPICT THE WINSOMELY POWER-
ful glory of God. Vast, open spaces of clean, white snow gleam at
the touch of the sun's light. Narwhals' horns emerge out of cracks
in the ice when they come up for air, and arctic foxes scurry and
jump headfirst into pillowy snow. The blizzards are an untamed
force, and the ice is a strong fortress.

What Are Fossil Fuels and Greenhouse Gases?

Fossil fuels are fossilized deposits of decayed plants and animals
(whose bodies contain carbon) heated and pressurized in the earth
over millennia. By burning fossil fuels like coal, oil, and natural gas
over centuries, we've altered the natural levels of heat-trapping
(greenhouse) gases in the atmosphere. Greenhouse gases act by
forming a "blanket" around the earth, warming the planet. Without
greenhouse gases—like carbon dioxide, methane, and water vapor—
our planet would be frozen and unsuitable for life. They're good and
necessary, in the right amounts.

The frozen poles appear almost otherworldly to us, but they are intimately intertwined with our ordinary lives, down to the wind we feel on our skin. Most of us don't live anywhere near the earth's poles, but wherever we live, we are connected to the polar realms by the climate. There's a global consensus: 97 percent of scientists agree that the earth's climate is changing at an unnatural rate, largely due to humanity's use of fossil fuels and the trapping of greenhouse gases in the atmosphere, and we are feeling the changes at home.[1]

CARBON EMISSIONS AND FOSSIL FUELS

Carbon dioxide and methane enter the air through cars, trains, planes, boats, industrial plants, agricultural practices, and deforestation. The Industrial Revolution and use of fossil fuels advanced medicine, gave us electricity, allowed us to travel to new places, and so much more. But carbon emissions come at a cost.

"God's creation is . . . running a fever."

The planet has a natural way of cycling and balancing carbon: it's captured in plants and trees during photosynthesis, animals take it up by eating the plants, and it eventually returns to the ground as organic matter (a similar system occurs between the atmosphere and the ocean). Carbon *gradually* returns to the air through natural seepage from the crust and volcanic activity (which accounts for a meager 1 percent of carbon emissions).

However, humans are taking carbon from the ground (in the form of fossil fuels) and injecting it into the atmosphere at a level the natural world has never handled before. As Dr. Katharine Hayhoe, a devoted Christian and renowned climate scientist, says, "God's creation is . . . running a fever."[2] The aches and pains show up as melting ice sheets and rising sea levels, plus an increase in heat waves, droughts, storm intensity, flooding, and forest fires worldwide.

THE IMPACTS ON NATURE AND HUMANS

Satellites reveal the shrinking ice sheets of the Arctic. Ice naturally fluctuates with the seasons, but summer ice in the Arctic is shrinking more than 13 percent each decade.[3] Summer ice is already naturally lower, but its lower limit is decreasing more and more each year. Where does the melted ice go? It shows up in our rising sea levels, which is a major problem for cities and communities whose buildings and homes are right on the coast.

→

The greenhouse effect is the natural warming of the earth's surface and atmosphere that results from the presence of carbon dioxide, methane, water vapor, and other gases or aerosols. Like a greenhouse, this radiating heat gets trapped in our atmosphere because certain gases allow sunlight to enter, while blocking the heat from escaping. Humans have augmented this greenhouse effect and interfered with the natural level of greenhouse gases in the atmosphere.

The Greenhouse Effect

NATURAL GREENHOUSE EFFECT

HUMAN GREENHOUSE EFFECT

SOLAR RADIATION

MORE HEAT ESCAPES INTO SPACE

LESS HEAT ESCAPES INTO SPACE

GREENHOUSE GASES

ATMOSPHERE

MORE GREENHOUSE GASES

CO_2

CH_4

N_2O

The vast, white surfaces of snow and ice in the polar areas help cool the earth by reflecting the sun's energy back into space. As we lose more ice cover at the poles, the white surface area is replaced by dark ocean waters, meaning our natural reflectors vanish. Instead, the waters absorb heat from the sun, like black asphalt on a summer day. The loss of the reflective ice intensifies the warming, and the problematic cycle progresses around the rest of the globe. The warming is further driven by deforestation as the loss of trees takes away one of our greatest means of absorbing carbon naturally from the air.

Other impacts—to our water supply, crop growth, and local temperatures—are already being witnessed and felt. The past decade was the hottest recorded in history.[4] Heat waves continue to climb in degree and days, and they're not just discomforting but deadly, especially for people without shelter or air-conditioning. Extreme weather events continually warn us of the trajectory we are on—in just half a decade a record-breaking five Atlantic hurricanes reached a category 5 level. A warming climate incites and intensifies wildfires from Australia to California, threatening homes and vital habitats. Climate change exacerbates existing problems of water scarcity, biodiversity loss, ocean acidification, coral bleaching, and low crop production yields. It turns up the dial on almost every environmental problem.

Satellites reveal the shrinking ice sheets of the Arctic.

A hotter planet affects our health too. Warmer temperatures are favorable to different diseases. Vector-borne disease-causing agents, or those carried by pests like mosquitoes and ticks (West Nile virus, Lyme disease, and dengue fever), are on the rise in North America. Water-borne diseases like cholera are also on the rise, as flooding and storm damage cause sewage issues and water contamination.

FOSSIL FUEL EXTRACTION: RISKY BUSINESS

Even without the changes accompanying a warming world, the methods we use to extract and ship fossil fuels are environmentally risky and often unsafe for workers. The pristine Arctic National Wildlife Refuge (ANWR) is the largest wilderness area in the US, home to indigenous tribes, a breeding ground for polar bears and caribou, and a habitat for more than two hundred other species like numerous migratory birds.[5] ANWR is threatened by oil industry efforts to take away protections and open the refuge to drilling.

Oil

The Keystone XL Pipeline project planned to carry oil 1,200 miles from Alberta in Canada to Nebraska in the US. After a controversial battle lasting over a decade, it was finally shut down in 2021, but similar pipeline projects are still in the works. Oil leaks and spills are an imminent threat on land and off our coasts. The 1989 Exxon Valdez oil tanker spill off Alaska's coast covered the Prince William Sound and miles of coastline with 11 million gallons of crude oil.

Fracking

Hydraulic fracking is a newer method that drills into the earth and injects high-pressure liquid into shale rock, breaking open fissures to extract gas and oil. In the US, it has grown domestic oil production and decreased gas prices. Fracking is water intensive; it can contaminate local water sources, and we're still unsure of the adverse effects it may have on seismic activity and earth tremors.[6]

A WAY FORWARD

One of the first things you can do is assess your carbon footprint. This will tell you where most of your personal greenhouse gas emissions are coming from and where you can make the biggest difference in lifestyle changes. There are many online tools available (like the EPA's online calculator) that will calculate your carbon footprint for you.

RENEWABLE ENERGY

There are still more than seven hundred million people around the world without electricity,[7] and energy is needed to improve life globally. But fossil fuels are not the way forward anymore. The economic benefits to drilling in new places and building expensive infrastructure to transport them aren't measuring up against the costs when cleaner, safer alternatives are available.

Clean energy, or renewable energy, comes from carbon-free sources, which are naturally replenished, like sunlight, wind, water, and geothermal heat. These options are promising and constantly improving and growing. Investing in, purchasing, and making clean energy available for developing countries is a worthy goal. The energy sector will create new jobs and businesses that are better for people and the planet. It's time to make this happen.

OUR PLANET'S NATURAL SOLUTION

Switching to renewable energy sources is half of the equation to solving global warming. It can halt our current emissions, but what do we do about the carbon dioxide that's already been released into the atmosphere? The answer is in the planet itself. The earth has natural mechanisms for absorbing and capturing carbon—wetlands, trees, plants, grass, seagrass, seaweed, kelp, and soil. These are all referred to as "carbon sinks." Vegetation captures carbon through photosynthesis, and microbes and fungi help break plants down, trapping the carbon in the soil. Reforesting the earth, restoring wetlands, protecting our kelp forests and seagrass beds, and switching to regenerative agriculture were solutions in earlier chapters, and now they're also the answer to our generation's biggest challenge: climate change. Be encouraged, we can do this! A planet of clear blues and verdant greens is our legacy and responsibility to future generations.

A BIBLICAL PERSPECTIVE

God designed our planet to be intricately connected within its large climate system, from pole to pole. What we do at home influences what happens at the poles and around the world. Here's the main moral issue at stake: it's impoverished communities, in developing countries especially, who suffer the most from everyone's lifestyle choices surrounding fossil fuel use. They're also less prepared with resources to deal with the hurricanes, fires, droughts, and floods exacerbated by climate change.

No matter the physical distance, we bear a responsibility for the fate of polar ecosystems and communities around the world enduring the burden of homes and habitats changing faster than they may be able to adapt. As Christians, we can't ignore the consequences of our daily decisions on others. We should be known as the meek who "will inherit the earth" (Matthew 5:5 NIV) and not the "destroyers of the earth" who greatly displease God (Revelation 11:18). Let's reduce our oil consumption, take real steps away from fossil fuels, support renewable energy, and work to rewild the world together.

Consult Your Conscience

If you're unsure about climate change, there are plenty of other reasons—air pollution, water quality, and oil drilling risks and disasters—to make the same changes toward clean energy. Consider what strikes you as compelling and important, then decide what changes you can make. Don't change your actions because you are alarmed; change them because you are convicted. Conviction is a steady, powerful motivator because it comes from love for God and His world.

The Redemption of Creation

Romans 8:22 reaffirms and reassures us that creation is a part of the redemptive finale we are headed to through Christ: "The whole creation has been groaning together in the pains of childbirth until now." We see this in the environmental disasters, disease outbreaks, diminishing polar ice, famines, and floods. Jesus came to earth initiating healing and restoration, and when we are fully redeemed at Christ's second coming, "creation itself will be set free from its bondage to corruption and obtain the freedom of the glory of the children of God" (v. 21). This is our hope. This is the grand scheme of the Gospel. The renewing Spirit will reach every ounce of the cosmos, from pole to pole, and creation's final, perfect redemption will be a knee-bending revealing of the glory of the Lord.

For now, when we step into our calling to be restored in Christ, we become restorers of our land and communities. The world needs to be encouraged to hope and believe in a God who is actively saving and redeeming. We have the opportunity, at such a time as this, when news is full of environmental problems and fear is running high, to step toward the issues that relieve suffering and walk beside a struggling world.

> The renewing Spirit will reach every ounce of the cosmos, from pole to pole, and creation's final, perfect redemption will be a knee-bending revealing of the glory of the Lord.

Our restorative work on earth today points us and others to our future home when Jesus comes again. Our future heaven on earth will be just as God planned, and all of creation can flourish without pain, corruption, or greed. No one will go hungry, and there will be no death. Instead, all of us, in our own ways, will find worship in all we do. This hope steadies us for the important work ahead of caring for the earth and its people, now until the coming of the new creation, world without end.

Reduce Your Carbon Footprint at Home

Most of our energy use happens in our homes—our heating, cooling, cooking, and washing. Small changes and energy-saving projects at home can cut carbon emissions and decrease utility costs.

CONDUCT A HOME ENERGY AUDIT.

▸ Many natural resources agencies and utility providers offer home energy audits that assess your energy consumption and analyze cost-effective ways to more efficiently use your energy at home and prevent energy waste.

INSULATE YOUR HOME TO PREVENT HEATING AND COOLING ENERGY WASTE.

▸ Effective home insulation prevents heating and cooling energy waste. It stops unwanted airflow in and out of our houses through windows, roofs, doors, walls, and floors, depending on the materials.

▸ For conventional thermostats, the Department of Energy (DOE) advises keeping the difference between the indoor and outdoor temperatures as small as possible.[8]

▸ Purchase a smart thermostat, which is more energy-efficient, lowers emissions, and reduces utility costs. It'll do the math for you!

REDUCE ENERGY USE FROM APPLIANCES.

▸ Dry laundry on a rack or clothesline instead of in the dryer.

▸ Turn off lights, hit the switch on power strips, and unplug electronics when not in use.

▸ Open windows or use a fan for as long as possible before turning on the AC.

▸ Again, cutting back on meat is a major help! Meat-heavy Western diets account for one-fifth of global emissions.[9]

▸ Cows pass loads of methane gas into the air, bless their hearts. Cattle ranching in places like Brazil is behind massive deforestation, and we need those trees to absorb carbon dioxide. The personal sacrifice of reducing your hamburger count or sourcing from ethical companies is worth it.

▸ If reducing your meat intake isn't an option for you, then purchase from regenerative farms whose livestock are managed in a way that helps the soil capture carbon.

PRACTICE CLIMATE-FRIENDLY LAWN MANAGEMENT.

▸ Plant trees, shrubs, and other native plants in your yard. All plants remove carbon dioxide from the air and store it in their roots, leaves, wood, and stems.

▸ Fruit trees and berry bushes offer fresh food to harvest right from your yard. It's wholesome, fun, and helpful for the climate!

▸ According to the US Forest Service, trees remove 10 to 20 percent of the annual fossil fuel emissions in the US.[10] There are carbon capture technologies in the works, but we have natural carbon capturers in our trees!

Make Transportation Choices to Lower Your Carbon Footprint

We are often on the move between home, work, errands, and school. Mobility is engrained in our lives, and it's a gift. We can pick up habits and make transportation decisions that reduce emissions and lead by example for others to follow.

REDUCE YOUR FLIGHTS.

- ▸ Travel by plane only when necessary, and attend conferences or meetings through online platforms when available.

- ▸ Many airlines now provide the option for travelers to offset their emissions from the flight with a small fee that goes toward emissions-reducing projects.

- ▸ Purchase carbon offsets (or climate credits) through initiatives like Reformation, Native, and Terrapass. The funds are directed toward projects actively reducing carbon dioxide in the atmosphere.

BIKE OFTEN.

- ▸ Biking is a healthy, active, zero-emissions alternative to driving. Bike to work, school, and other close destinations.

USE PUBLIC TRANSPORTATION OR CARPOOL.

- ▸ Carpool with your neighbors, classmates, and colleagues to and from work, school, and other errands. Fewer cars on the road means less emissions.

- ▸ Take the bus, subway, metro, or rail when possible.

DRIVE ELECTRIC VEHICLES (EV).

- ▸ EVs always reduce greenhouse gas emissions, especially when the electricity source is renewable, and they are increasingly more feasible and affordable.

- ▸ If you switch from a gasoline-powered car to an electric car, emissions can be reduced by 50 percent if the EV is powered by the conventional grid, and by 95 percent if powered by solar energy.[11]

Use Renewable Energy Options to Lower Your Carbon Footprint

All our energy use at home can contribute to greenhouse gas emissions unless we choose to make the switch to renewables. The US electricity supply is separated into conventional energy (coal, nuclear, oil, and natural gas) and renewable energy or green power (sources that are continually replenished over time without becoming depleted).

SWITCH TO GREEN POWER IN YOUR HOME.

- ▶ Electricity production accounts for 25 percent of greenhouse gas emissions globally.[12]

- ▶ Some major renewable options with promising growth and availability are solar power, wind energy, and geothermal energy.

- ▶ Find out if your state's retail electricity market is traditionally regulated or competitive. You may be able to choose your electricity provider based on the renewable energy options they provide.

- ▶ A helpful source is the Green-e website, which includes certified and verified green power options by state.

- ▶ Install solar panels at your home. Look into the local, state, and federal incentives for solar power in your region. Lead by example in your neighborhood with renewable generation right on your property.

Advocate to Speed Up the Transition to Renewable Energy

While our personal energy habits matter, the energy system at large is like a giant machine that's been running off fossil fuels for decades. There are challenges to overcome in transitioning from the oil reserves to renewable sources, but we can advocate for a just and prompt transition to clean energy.

SECURE JOBS IN RENEWABLE ENERGY FOR DISPLACED FOSSIL FUEL WORKERS.

- ► Those who earn their livelihoods from the conventional energy sector can be trained and prepared for the shift toward clean energy development. Advocate for policies that make provisions for workers during the transition.

- ► Encourage your local, state, and federal leaders to incentivize the construction of new energy-efficient homes, the installation of new EV charging stations, and the sealing of leaking oil and gas wells to create millions of new jobs.

OPPOSE OFFSHORE OIL AND GAS PROJECTS.

- ► Halting new leases for offshore oil and gas could prevent the release of more than nineteen billion tons of greenhouse gases into the atmosphere.[13]

- ► Research and learn about fracking, drilling, and other fossil fuel actions near your area. When energy projects are awaiting permission to proceed, you can challenge whether they are needed and beneficial to the community and whether the funds and efforts would be better directed toward cleaner options.

STAND UP FOR PARIS AGREEMENT COMMITMENTS.

- ► Under the Paris Agreement, the US committed to cut emissions by half, compared to 2005 levels, by the end of this decade. We need to do our best to keep our word and lead by example, especially as a people responsible for a major percentage of emissions to date. Let your representatives know that you care about your country's performance and leadership in reducing emissions promptly.

TALK ABOUT CLIMATE CHANGE ISSUES.

- ► Watch documentaries or listen to podcasts with friends and family and discuss what you think together. Some podcasts to check out: *How to Save a Planet, Hot Take, Drilled, Yale Climate Connections,* and *Warming Signs.*

- Check out Dr. Katharine Hayhoe's "Global Weirding" YouTube channel for clear and helpful insights into the questions and issues. Become informed so you'll be more equipped to share and help others process and make changes too.

Clean Up Oil Spills

Pipeline ruptures, drilling operation explosions, and oil tanker shipwrecks can all end in oil spill disasters. Sea otters, sea turtles, pelicans, dolphins, whales, and many other marine creatures become coated in the oil or ingest it, leading to hypothermia, poisoning, suffocation, and often death. Oil spills tragically disrupt ecosystems and fishing and tourist economies, and recovery can take decades.

SUPPORT OIL SPILL CLEANUPS.

- The US Coast Guard holds the primary responsibility for cleaning up oil spills with the scientific guidance and support of NOAA. Follow NOAA's "Eyes in the Sky Surveilling for Pollution" project, which publishes oil spills in near–real time online.

- Cleaning oil from an environment requires professional training and skill because people can end up causing additional damage even when trying to help. Only trained personnel should rescue and rehabilitate marine species.

- When spills happen, volunteers may be needed to pick up trash and other debris before the major oil cleanup begins, help clean equipment, or help with administrative work. Check out state-run volunteer programs, NOAA, and the U.S. Fish and Wildlife Service for opportunities if a spill occurs.

- Oil persists in the environment after initial cleanup, requiring restoration projects to recover fully. Check out NOAA's "Restoration Atlas" for coastal restoration projects near you.

Support Nonprofits Working on Climate Action

- **World Relief** focuses on clean energy, community building, and climate refugees (communities displaced by sea level rise, drought, and other climate-related crises).

- **Convoy of Hope** works in disaster relief and preparedness.

- **World Renew** aids in natural disaster response, clean energy, and food insecurity with a focus on family-centered community development.

- To get involved in faith-based climate policy advocacy, check out the **Evangelical Environmental Network** and **YECA (Young Evangelicals For Climate Action)**.

NOTES

Chapter 1: Fresh Water

1. "1 in 3 People Globally Do Not Have Access to Safe Drinking Water—UNICEF, WHO," World Health Organization, June 18, 2019, https://www.who.int/news /item/18–06–2019-1-in-3-people-globally-do-not-have-access-to-safe-drinking -water-unicef-who.

2. "QuickFacts: Flint City, Michigan," United States Census Bureau, accessed August, 26, 2021, https://www.census.gov/quickfacts/fact/table/flintcitymichigan /PST045219.

3. Melissa Denchak, "Flint Water Crisis: Everything You Need to Know," NRDC.org, November 8, 2018, https://www.nrdc.org/stories/flint-water-crisis-everything -you-need-know.

4. Meera Subramanian, "India's Terrifying Water Crisis," *New York Times*, July 15, 2019, https://www.nytimes.com/2019/07/15/opinion/india-water-crisis.html.

5. Anthony Acciavatti, "The Ganges Water Crisis," *New York Times*, June 17, 2015, https://www.nytimes.com/2015/06/18/opinion/the-ganges-water-crisis.html?ref =international&_r=0; Simon Scarr, Weiyi Cai, Vinod Kumar, and Alasdair Pal, "The Race to Save the River Ganges," Reuters.com, January 18, 2019, https://graphics .reuters.com/INDIA-RIVER/010081TW39P/index.html.

6. "Xeriscaping," *National Geographic*, last updated January 21, 2011, https://www. nationalgeographic.org/encyclopedia/xeriscaping/.

Chapter 2: Endangered Species

1. Sandra Díaz et al., "Summary for Policymakers of the Global Assessment Report on Biodiversity and Ecosystem Services of the Intergovernmental Science-Policy Platform on Biodiversity and Ecosystem Services," IPBES, 2019, https://ipbes.net /sites/default/files/2020–02/ipbes_global_assessment_report_summary_for _policymakers_en.pdf.

2. Sandra Díaz et al., "Summary for Policymakers of the Global Assessment Report

on Biodiversity and Ecosystem Services of the Intergovernmental Science-Policy Platform on Biodiversity and Ecosystem Services," IPBES, 2019, https://ipbes.net /sites/default/files/2020–02/ipbes_global_assessment_report_summary_for _policymakers_en.pdf.

3. Gerardo Ceballos, Paul R. Ehrlich, and Peter H. Raven, "Vertebrates on the Brink as Indicators of Biological Annihilation and the Sixth Mass Extinction," *PNAS* 117, no. 24 (June 2020): 13596–13602, https://doi.org/ 10.1073/pnas.1922686117.

4. "Tigers Only Found in Zoos by 2030?" Endangered Species International. https:// www.endangeredspeciesinternational.org/tigers.html. Accessed September 2021.

5. Kate Garibaldi, "Sea Otters," Defenders of Wildlife, Accessed September 2021, https://defenders.org/wildlife/sea-otter.

6. "Snow Leopard Range Map," Snow Leopard Conservancy, 2011, https:// snowleopardconservancy.org/text/how/range.htm; "Action for Snow Leopards," IUCN, August 14, 2020, https://www.iucn.org/news/eastern-europe-and -central-asia/202008/action-snow-leopards.

7. "Threats to African Elephants," World Wildlife Fund, accessed August 26, 2021, https://wwf.panda.org/discover/knowledge_hub/endangered_species/elephants /african_elephants/afelephants_threats/?.

8. "Poaching for Rhino Horn," Save the Rhino, accessed August 26, 2021, https:// www.savetherhino.org/rhino-info/threats/poaching-rhino-horn/.

9. Muhammad Adnan Shereen, Suliman Khan, Abeer Kazmi, Nadia Bashir, and Rabeea Siddique, "COVID-19 Infection: Emergence, Transmission, and Characteristics of Human Coronaviruses," *Journal of Advanced Research* 24 (July 2020): 91–98, https://doi.org/10.1016/j.jare.2020.03.005.

10. Ping Liu et al., **"Are Pangolins the Intermediate Host of the 2019 Novel Coronavirus (SARS-CoV-2)?"** *PLOS Pathogens* 16, no. 5 (May 2020): e1008421, https://doi.org/10.1371/journal.ppat.1008421.

11. "Giant Goldfish Problem in US Lake Prompts Warning to Pet Owners," BBC News, July 13, 2021, https://www.bbc.com/news/world-us-canada-57816922.

12. US Wildlife Trafficking Alliance, US Fish & Wildlife Service, World Wildlife Fund, and TRAFFIC, *Caribbean Traveler's Guide*, https://www.fws.gov/international/pdf /caribbean-buyer-beware-brochure.pdf.

13. Mitch Merry, "5 Things You Can Do to Help Protect the Endangered Species Act," Endangered Species Coalition, February 21, 2017, https://www.endangered.org /5-things-you-can-do-to-help-protect-the-endangered-species-act/.

Chapter 3: Mountains and Minerals

1. "Rocks and Minerals: Everyday Uses," Museum of Natural and Cultural History, accessed August 26, 2021, https://mnch.uoregon.edu/rocks-and-minerals -everyday-uses.

2. Megan R. Nichols, "5 Ways to Make Mining More Sustainable," Empowering

Pumps and Equipment, February 18, 2020, https://empoweringpumps.com/5-ways-to-make-mining-more-sustainable/.

3. "Green Mining," Mission 2016: The Future of Strategic Natural Resources, MIT, 2016, https://web.mit.edu/12.000/www/m2016/finalwebsite/solutions/greenmining.html.

4. Michael Standaert, "China Wrestles with the Toxic Aftermath of Rare Earth Mining," *Yale Environment 360*, July 2, 2019, https://e360.yale.edu/features/china-wrestles-with-the-toxic-aftermath-of-rare-earth-mining.

5. Richard Schiffman, "A Troubling Look at the Human Toll of Mountaintop Removal Mining," *Yale Environment 360*, November 21, 2017, https://e360.yale.edu/features/a-troubling-look-at-the-human-toll-of-mountaintop-removal-mining; Sarah Saadoun, "The Coal Mine Next Door: How the US Government's Deregulation of Mountaintop Removal Threatens Public Health," Human Rights Watch, December 10, 2018, https://www.hrw.org/report/2018/12/10/coal-mine-next-door/how-us-governments-deregulation-mountaintop-removal-threatens.

6. "Behind the Bling: Forced and Child Labour in the Jewellery Industry," World Vision Australia, accessed September 7, 2021, https://www.worldvision.com.au/docs/default-source/buy-ethical-fact-sheets/7185_dtl_factsheet_jewellery_lr.pdf?sfvrsn=2.

7. "Electronics Donation and Recycling," Environmental Protection Agency, accessed August 26, 2021, https://www.epa.gov/recycle/electronics-donation-and-recycling.

8. Jo Becker and Juliane Kippenberg, "The Hidden Cost of Jewelry: Human Rights in Supply Chains and the Responsibility of Jewelry Companies," Human Rights Watch, February 8, 2018, https://www.hrw.org/report/2018/02/08/hidden-cost-jewelry/human-rights-supply-chains-and-responsibility-jewelry.

9. Becker and Kippenberg, "The Hidden Cost of Jewelry."

Chapter 4: Air and Sky

1. National Geographic Society, "Light Pollution," *National Geographic*, July 23, 2019, https://www.nationalgeographic.org/article/light-pollution/.

2. "Visibility and Regional Haze," Environmental Protection Agency, accessed August 26, 2021, https://www.epa.gov/visibility.

3. United Nations Environment Programme, "Towards a Pollution-Free Planet: Background Report," UN Environment, September 2017, https://wedocs.unep.org/bitstream/handle/20.500.11822/21800/UNEA_towardspollution_long%20version_Web.pdf?sequence=1&isAllowed=y.

4. Bruce Bekkar, MD; Susan Pacheco, MD; Rupa Basu, PhD; et al, "Association of Air Pollution and Heat Exposure with Preterm Birth, Low Birth Weight, and Stillbirth in the US," *Journal of the American Medical Association*, published June 18, 2020, https://jamanetwork.com/journals/jamanetworkopen/fullarticle/2767260?utm_source=For_The_Media&utm_medium=referral&utm_campaign=ftm_links&utm_term=061820.

5. Rachel M. Shaffer, Magali N. Blango, Ge Li, Sara D. Adar, Marco Carone, Adam A. Szpiro, Joel D. Kaufman, Timothy V. Larson, Eric B. Larson, Paul K. Crane, and Lianne Sheppard, "Fine Particulate Matter and Dementia Incidence in the Adult Changes in Thought Study," *Environmental Health Perspectives*, Vol. 129, No. 8, Published August 4, 2021, https://ehp.niehs.nih.gov/doi/10.1289/EHP9018.

6. "Air Pollution," WHO, accessed August 26, 2021, https://www.who.int/health-topics/air-pollution#tab=tab_1.

7. "Air Pollution," WHO.

8. Marcel Theroux, "The World's Dirtiest Air," Unreported World, April 29, 2018, YouTube video, 23:50, https://youtu.be/kUNuHxrd7Y0.

9. "Air Pollution," WHO.

10. "Air Pollution," WHO.

11. Miranda Green, "EPA Scientists Find Black Communities Disproportionately Hit by Pollution," *The Hill*, February 23, 2018, https://thehill.com/policy/energy-environment/375289-epa-scientists-find-emissions-greater-impact-low-income-communities.

12. Jeff McMahon, "Electric Vehicles Cost Less Than Half as Much to Drive," *Forbes*, January 14, 2018, https://www.forbes.com/sites/jeffmcmahon/2018/01/14/electric-vehicles-cost-less-than-half-as-much-to-drive/?sh=27775ec23f97.

Chapter 5: Woodlands

1. "UN Report: Nature's Dangerous Decline 'Unprecedented'; Species Extinction Rates 'Accelerating,'" *Sustainable Development Goals* (blog), UN, May 6, 2019, https://www.un.org/sustainabledevelopment/blog/2019/05/nature-decline-unprecedented-report/.

2. "Yale Experts Explain Healthy Forests," Yale Office of Sustainability, December 16, 2020, https://sustainability.yale.edu/explainers/yale-experts-explain-healthy-forests?utm_source=YaleToday&utm_medium=Email&utm_campaign=YT_YaleToday-Students_12–22–2020.

3. Mikaela Weisse and Elizabeth Dow Goldman, "We Lost a Football Pitch of Primary Rainforest Every 6 Seconds in 2019," World Resources Institute, June 2, 2020, https://www.wri.org/insights/we-lost-football-pitch-primary-rainforest-every-6-seconds-2019.

4. "Forests and Poverty Reduction," Food and Agriculture Organization of the United Nations, last updated May 15, 2015, http://www.fao.org/forestry/livelihoods/en/.

5. "Deforestation and Forest Degradation," World Wildlife Fund, accessed August 26, 2021, https://www.worldwildlife.org/threats/deforestation-and-forest-degradation.

6. Domingos Cardoso et al., "Amazon Plant Diversity Revealed by a Taxonomically Verified Species List," PNAS 114, no. 40 (October 2017): 10695–10700, https://doi.org/10.1073/pnas.1706756114.

7. *Encyclopedia Britannica*, s.v. "Amazon Rainforest," accessed August 27, 2021, https://www.britannica.com/place/Amazon-Rainforest.

8. "Deforestation and Forest Degradation," World Wildlife Fund.

9. Gregory S. Cooper, Simon Willcock, and John A. Dearing, "Regime Shifts Occur Disproportionately Faster in Larger Ecosystems," Nature Communications 11, no. 1175 (March 2020), https://doi.org/10.1038/s41467-020-15029-x.

10. Fen Montaigne, "Will Deforestation and Warming Push the Amazon to a Tipping Point?" *Yale Environment 360*, September 4, 2019, https://e360.yale.edu/features/will-deforestation-and-warming-push-the-amazon-to-a-tipping-point; Carlos A. Nobre et al., "Land-use and Climate Change Risks in the Amazon and the Need of a Novel Sustainable Development Paradigm," PNAS 113, no. 39 (September 2016): 10759–10768, https://doi.org/10.1073/pnas.1605516113.

11. Robert Toovey Walker et al., "Avoiding Amazonian Catastrophes: Prospects for Conservation in the 21st Century," *One Earth*, vol. 1, no. 2 (October 2019): 202–215, https://doi.org/10.1016/j.oneear.2019.09.009.

12. Tree of Life," Bible Project, accessed August 27, 2021, https://bibleproject.com/learn/tree-of-life/.

13. Gabrielle Kissinger, Martin Herold, and Veronique De Sy, "Drivers of Deforestation and Forest Degradation: A Synthesis Report for REDD+ Policymakers," Lexeme Consulting, August 2012, https://assets.publishing.service.gov.uk/government/uploads/system/uploads/attachment_data/file/65505/6316-drivers-deforestation-report.pdf.

14. "Fairtrade Four," Fairtrade America, accessed August 27, 2021, https://www.fairtradeamerica.org/for-media/fairtrade-four/.

15. "7 Everyday Foods from the Rainforest," Rainforest Alliance, last updated September 16, 2017, https://www.rainforest-alliance.org/articles/7-everyday-foods-from-the-rainforest.

16. "The Search for Sustainable Palm Oil," Rainforest Alliance, last updated August 5, 2019, https://www.rainforest-alliance.org/articles/search-for-sustainable-palm-oil.

17. "Recycling of Old Newspapers and Mechanical Papers Graph," American Forest & Paper Association, August 20, 2021, https://www.afandpa.org/statistics-resources/resources.

18. "Tropical Forests in Our Daily Lives," Rainforest Alliance, last updated December 5, 2017, https://www.rainforest-alliance.org/articles/tropical-forests-in-our-daily-lives.

Chapter 6: Soil

1. "24 Billion Tons of Fertile Land Lost Every Year, Warns UN Chief on World Day to Combat Desertification," *UN News*, June 16, 2019, https://news.un.org/en/story/2019/06/1040561.

2. Kevin Dennehey, "New Online Forest Atlas Tracks State of Global Forests," Yale School of the Environment, December 18, 2014, https://environment.yale.edu /news/article/new-online-forest atlas-to-share-story-of-resources-worldwide/.

3. David Pimentel, "Soil Erosion: A Food and Environmental Threat," *Journal of the Environment, Development and Sustainability*, 8 (February 2006): 119–137, https://doi .org/10.1007/s10668–005–1262–8.

4. "Part 1: Food Security and Nutrition Around the World in 2020," Food and Agriculture Organization of the UN, accessed August 27, 2021, http://www.fao .org/3/ca9692en/online/ca9692en.html#chapter-1_1.

5. "Part 1: Food Security and Nutrition," Food and Agriculture Organization of the UN, http://www.fao.org/3/ca9692en/online/ca9692en.html#chapter-1_1.

6. Eric Holt-Giménez, Annie Shattuck, Miguel A. Altieri, Steve Gliessman, and Hans Herren, "We Already Grow Enough Food for 10 Billion People . . . and Still Can't End Hunger," *Journal of Sustainable Agriculture,* vol. 36, no. 6 (July 2012): 595–598, https://doi.org/10.1080/10440046.2012.695331.

7. H. Charles J. Godfray et al., "Food Security: The Challenge of Feeding 9 Billion People," *Science*, vol. 327, no. 5967 (February 2010): 812–818, https://doi.org /10.1126/science.1185383.

8. "Worldwide Food Waste," United Nations Environment Programme, Accessed September 2021, https://www.unep.org/thinkeatsave/get-informed /worldwide-food-waste.

9. "Food Waste in America in 2021: Statistics and Facts," RTS, accessed August 27, 2021, https://www.rts.com/resources/guides/food-waste-america/.

10. "Grocery Industry Launches New Initiative to Reduce Consumer Confusion on Product Date Labels," Consumer Brands Association, February 15, 2017, https:// consumerbrandsassociation.org/posts/grocery-industry-launches-new-initiative-to -reduce-consumer-confusion-on-product-date-labels/.

11. "Facts and Figures about Materials, Waste and Recycling: Nondurable Goods: Product-Specific Data," United States Environmental Protection agency, Last Updated August 26, 2021, https://www.epa.gov/facts-and-figures-about -materials-waste-and-recycling/nondurable-goods-product-specific-data #ClothingandFootwear.

12. "The Impact of a Cotton Tshirt: How smart choices can make a difference in our water and energy footprint," World Wildlife Fund, January 16, 2013, https://www .worldwildlife.org/stories/the-impact-of-a-cotton-t-shirt. Accessed September 2021.

Chapter 7: Pollinators

1. Simon G. Potts et al., "Summary for Policymakers of the Assessment Report of the Intergovernmental Science-Policy Platform on Biodiversity and Ecosystem Services on Pollinators, Pollination and Food Production" (Bonn, Germany: IPBES, 2016), https://ipbes.net/sites/default/files/spm_deliverable_3a_pollination_20170222.pdf.

Notes

2. Jeff Ollerton, Rachael Winfree, and Sam Tarrant, "How Many Flowering Plants Are Pollinated by Animals?" Oikos 120, no. 3 (March 2011): 321–326, https://doi.org/10.1111/j.1600–0706.2010.18644.x.

3. Caspar A. Hallmann et al., "More Than 75 Percent Decline Over 27 Years in Total Flying Insect Biomass in Protected Areas, *PLOS* ONE 12, no. 10 (October 2017): e0185809, https://doi.org/10.1371/journal.pone.0185809.

4. Francisco Sánchez-Bayo and Kris Wyckhuys, "Worldwide Decline of the Entomofauna: A Review of Its Drivers," *Biological Conservation* 232 (April 2019): 8–27, https://doi.org/10.1016/j.biocon.2019.01.020.

5. Jamie Ellis, "The Honey Bee Crisis," Outlooks on Pest Management 23, no. 1 (February 2012): 35–40, https://doi.org/10.1564/22feb10.

6. Laura A. Burkle, John C. Marlin, and Tiffany M. Knight, "Plant-Pollinator Interactions over 120 Years: Loss of Species, Co-Occurrence, and Function," *Science*, March 29, 2013, Vol. 339, Issue 6127, pp. 1611–15, https://www.science.org/lookup/doi/10.1126/science.1232728.

7. Sarina Jepsen et al., *Conservation Status and Ecology of Monarchs in the United States* (Arlington, VA and Portland, OR: NatureServe and the Xerces Society, 2015), https://www.natureserve.org/sites/default/files/news-items/files/natureserve-xerces_monarchs_usfs-final.pdf.

8. "Bat Pollination," US Forest Service, accessed August 27, 2021, https://www.fs.fed.us/wildflowers/pollinators/animals/bats.shtml.

9. Christian Schwägerl, "What's Causing the Sharp Decline in Insects, and Why It Matters," *Yale Environment 360*, July 6, 2016, https://e360.yale.edu/features/insect_numbers_declining_why_it_matters.

10. "Passion for Pollinators," Illinois Department of Natural Resources, accessed September 2021, https://www2.illinois.gov/dnr/education/Pages/PollinatorMain.aspx.

11. Susannah B. Lerman, Alexandra R. Contosta, Joan Milam, and Christofer Bang, "To Mow or to Mow Less: Lawn Mowing Frequency Affects Bee Abundance and Diversity in Suburban Yards," *Biological Conservation*, vol. 221 (May 2018): 160–174, https://doi.org/10.1016/j.biocon.2018.01.025.

12. "Monarch Waystation Program," Monarch Watch, accessed August 27, 2021, https://www.monarchwatch.org/waystations/.

13. Leonard Perry, "Beneficial Nematodes," University of Vermont, Department of Plant and Soil Science, accessed August 27, 2021, https://pss.uvm.edu/ppp/articles/nemat.html.

Chapter 8: Wetlands

1. Natural Resources Conservation Service, "Restoring America's Wetlands: A Private Lands Conservation Success Story," USDA, accessed August 27, 2021, https://www.nrcs.usda.gov/Internet/FSE_DOCUMENTS/stelprdb1045079.pdf.

2. "Wetlands Disappearing Three Times Faster Than Forests," UN Climate Change

News, October 1, 2018, https://unfccc.int/news/wetlands-disappearing-three-times-faster-than-forests.

3. "Wetlands Disappearing Three Times Faster," UN Climate Change News.

4. "Wetlands Disappearing Three Times Faster," UN Climate Change News.

5. "Coastal Wetlands: Too Valuable to Lose," National Oceanic and Atmospheric Administration, last updated January 22, 2021, https://www.fisheries.noaa.gov/national/habitat-conservation/coastal-wetlands-too-valuable-lose.

6. "Conserving Wetlands & Waterfowl: Science, Research and a Strong Biological Foundation," Ducks Unlimited, accessed August 27, 2021, https://www.ducks.org/conservation/how-du-conserves-wetlands-and-waterfowl.

Chapter 9: Coral Reefs

1. "Shallow Coral Reef Habitat," National Oceanic and Atmospheric Administration, last updated January 21, 2020, https://www.fisheries.noaa.gov/national/habitat-conservation/shallow-coral-reef-habitat.

2. National Institute for Mathematical and Biological Synthesis (NIMBioS), "Study Projects Unprecedented Loss of Corals in Great Barrier Reef Due to Warming," ScienceDaily, January 22, 2015, https://www.sciencedaily.com/releases/2015/01/150122103242.htm.

3. "Coral Reef Ecosystems," National Oceanic and Atmospheric Administration, last updated February 1, 2019, https://www.noaa.gov/education/resource-collections/marine-life/coral-reef-ecosystems.

4. Terry P. Hughes et al., "Ecological Memory Modifies the Cumulative Impact of Recurrent Climate Extremes," *Nature Climate Change* 9 (2019): 40–43, https://doi.org/10.1038/s41558–018–0351–2; Andreas Dietzel, Michael Bode, Sean R. Connolly, and Terry P. Hughes, "Long-Term Shifts in the Colony Size Structure of Coral Populations Along the Great Barrier Reef," *Proceedings of the Royal Society B: Biological Sciences* 287, no. 1936 (October 2020), https://doi.org/10.1098/rspb.2020.1432.

5. "Coral Reef Ecosystems," National Oceanic and Atmospheric Administration.

6. "Coral Reef Ecosystems," National Oceanic and Atmospheric Administration.

7. Robert Brumbaugh, "Healthy Coral Reefs Are Good for Tourism—And Tourism Can Be Good for Reefs," World Economic Forum, June 21, 2017, https://www.weforum.org/agenda/2017/06/healthy-coral-reefs-are-good-for-tourism-and-tourism-can-be-good-for-reefs/.

8. "Managing Wastewater to Support Coral Reef Health, Resilience," UN Environment Programme, November 27, 2018, https://www.unenvironment.org/fr/node/23977.

Chapter 10: The Ocean

1. Roland Geyer, Jenna R. Jambeck, and Kara Lavender Law, "Production, Use, and Fate of All Plastics Ever Made," *Science*, vol. 3, no. 7, (July 2017): e1700782, https://doi.org/10.1126/sciadv.1700782.

2. "The New Plastics Economy: Rethinking the Future of Plastics," World Economic Forum, January 2016, http://www3.weforum.org/docs/WEF_The_New_Plastics _Economy.pdf.

3. Alexandra Simon-Lewis, "Humans Have Generated One Billion Elephants Worth of Plastic," *Wired*, July 19, 2017, https://www.wired.co.uk/article/global-total -plastic-waste-oceans.

4. Chris Wilcox, Erik Van Sebille, and Britta Denise Hardesty, "Threat of Plastic Pollution to Seabirds Is Global, Pervasive, and Increasing," PNAS 112, no. 38 (August 2015): 11899–11904, https://doi.org/10.1073/pnas.1502108112.

5. Emily M. Duncan et al., "Microplastic Ingestion Ubiquitous in Marine Turtles," *Global Change Biology*, vol. 25, no. 2 (February 2019): 744–752, https://doi.org /10.1111/gcb.14519.

6. Chelsea M. Rochman et al., "Anthropogenic Debris in Seafood: Plastic Debris and Fibers from Textiles in Fish and Bivalves Sold for Human Consumption," Scientific Reports 5 (2015), https://doi.org/10.1038/srep14340.

7. "Ocean Acidification," National Oceanic and Atmospheric Administration, last updated April 1, 2020, https://www.noaa.gov/education/resource-collections /ocean-coasts/ocean-acidification.

8. *The State of World Fisheries and Aquaculture 2016: Contributing to Food Security and Nutrition for All* (Rome: FAO, 2016), http://www.fao.org/3/i5555e/i5555e.pdf.

9. "Why Should We Care About the Ocean?" National Ocean Service, NOAA, accessed August 27, 2021, https://oceanservice.noaa.gov/facts/why-care-about -ocean.html.

10. "Ocean & Coasts," National Oceanic and Atmospheric Administration, last updated August 24, 2021, https://www.noaa.gov/oceans-coasts.

11. Jenna R. Jambeck, et al., "Plastic Waste Input from Land into the Ocean." *Science*, vol. 347, no. 6223, pp. 768–771, https://science.sciencemag.org/content/347 /6223/768.full. Accessed 22 March 2021.

12. "Top Ten Items," Ocean Conservancy, May 9, 2017, https://oceanconservancy.org /news/top-ten-items/.

Chapter 11: The Poles and Global Climate

1. https://iopscience.iop.org/article/10.1088/1748-9326/11/4/048002

2. Ann Neumann, "Katharine Hayhoe: God's Creation Is Running a Fever," *Guernica*, December 15, 2014, https://www.guernicamag.com/gods-creation-is-running -a-fever/.

3. Richard L. Thomas, Jacqueline Richter-Menge, and Matthew L. Druckenmiller, eds., Arctic Report Card 2020 (NOAA, 2020), https://arctic.noaa.gov/Portals/7 /ArcticReportCard/Documents/ArcticReportCard_full_report2020.pdf.

4. Matt McGrath, "Climate Change: Last Decade Confirmed As Warmest on Record," BBC, January 15, 2020, https://www.bbc.com/news/science-environment-51111176;

"Climate Dashboard," Met Office, accessed August 28, 2021, https://www.metoffice
.gov.uk/hadobs/monitoring/dashboard.html; "NASA, NOAA Analyses Reveal 2019
Second Warmest Year on Record," NASA, January 15, 2020, https://www.nasa
.gov/press-release/nasa-noaa-analyses-reveal-2019-second-warmest-year-on-record.

5. "Wildlife & Habitat," US Fish & Wildlife Service, last updated November 5, 2013,
https://www.fws.gov/refuge/arctic/wildlife_habitat.html.

6. John Wihbey, "Pros and Cons of Fracking: 5 Key Issues," Yale Climate
Connections, May 27, 2015, https://yaleclimateconnections.org/2015/05/pros-and
-cons-of-fracking-5-key-issues/.

7. "SDG7: Data and Projections," International Energy Association, October 2020,
https://www.iea.org/reports/sdg7-data-and-projections.

8. "Thermostats," Department of Energy, accessed August 27, 2021, https://www
.energy.gov/energysaver/thermostats.

9. "Plant-Rich Diets," Project Drawdown, accessed August 27, 2021, https://
drawdown.org/solutions/plant-rich-diets.

10. Stephen R. Shifley et al., "Criterion 5: Maintenance of Forest Contributions to
Global Carbon Cycles," in Forests of the Northern United States (Newtown Square,
PA: USDA Forest Service Northern Research Station, 2012), 74–78, https://www
.fs.fed.us/nrs/pubs/gtr/gtr_nrs90/gtr-nrs-90-chapter-5.5.pdf?.

11. "Electric Cars," Project Drawdown, accessed August 28, 2021, https://drawdown.org
/solutions/electric-cars.

12. "Electricity," Project Drawdown, accessed August 28, 2021, https://drawdown.org
/sectors/electricity.

13. "Offshore Drilling Fuels the Climate Crisis and Threatens the Economy," Oceana,
January 2021, https://usa.oceana.org/publications/reports/offshore-drilling
-fuels-climate-crisis-and-threatens-economy.

INFOGRAPHICS FACTS
AND FIGURES

The Endangerment of Tigers

- ▶ "Sunda Tiger," World Wildlife Fund, accessed September 2021, https://www. worldwildlife.org/species/sunda-tiger.
- ▶ "Tiger," World Wildlife Day, accessed September 2021, https://wildlifeday.org /content/factsheets/tiger.
- ▶ "Tigers," Save Animals Facing Extinction, accessed September 2021, https://saveanimalsfacingextinction.org/animals/tigers/.

The Formation of Minerals and Gemstones

- ▶ "How Do Gemstones Form?" Gem Rock Auctions, accessed September 2021, https://www.gemrockauctions.com/learn/technical-information-on-gemstones /how-do-gemstones-form.

Global Food Production and Waste

- ▶ "8 Facts to Know About Food Waste and Hunger," World Food Program USA, August 10, 2021. https://www.wfpusa.org/articles/8-facts-to-know-about-food -waste-and-hunger/.
- ▶ "Worldwide Food Waste," United Nations Environment Programme, accessed September 2021, https://www.unep.org/thinkeatsave/get-informed/worldwide -food-waste.

The Importance of Pollinators

- ▶ Emily Hoskins, "Pollinators by Number," Green Bee, June 11, 2019, https://greenbeeohio.com/pollinators-by-number/.
- ▶ "Pollinator Friendly Cookbook," Pollinator Partnership, accessed September 2021, https://www.pollinator.org/pollinated-food.
- ▶ "Pollinators Need You. You Need Pollinators." Pollinator Partnership, accessed September 2021, https://www.pollinator.org/pollinators.

ACKNOWLEDGMENTS

MOM, THANK YOU FOR TEACHING ME HOW TO CARE FOR ANIMALS with gentleness and love. I'll never forget the trail of marshmallows you made for the raccoons in the front yard (not the best wildlife management tactic, but I love you for it). Dad, thanks for encouraging me to start brainstorming and writing this book early on. Both of you have supported my scientific studies and my heart for God in complementary ways; you are the parental dream team!

I also want to thank Esther, my roommate and sister-friend. Thanks for constantly encouraging me up the mountain of writing a book, and for envisioning me steadily jogging up it in a white jumpsuit. I'm still not sure what that means, but it sure was an empowering image.

Shout out as well to my COVID pod: Claire, Lize, Tim, Michael, Tristan, Justina, and Mike. You guys kept me (mostly) sane with your companionship, laughter, and many celebrations along the milestone moments of creating this book during a pandemic. Long live the Tent Fort.

Many thanks to all my Yale professors: Professor Hare (for reminding me, in the words of Julian of Norwich, "all shall be well, and all manner of things shall be well."); Professor Gordon (for opening up the narratives of the history of the Christian faith, especially the relationship between faith and science); Professor Eitel (for your wisdom, guidance, and encouragement in my writing and theological studies); Professor Berger (for encouraging an engagement with all of creation in praise of God); Professor Mary Beth Decker (for your insights into the Oceans chapter and helping me wrap my mind around the ocean's circulation and its biological implications); Professor Shimi (for yeeting that crab across the marsh when it pinched you and greatly caring that we learn about coastal ecosystems); and Professor Freidenburg (for your insights into the Wetlands chapter and your enthusiasm for this project before I was even your student).

Special thanks to my writing professors, Verlyn Klinkenborg and Chris Wiman. Verlyn, thank you for your honest critiques that sharpened my writing and my faith. Chris, thanks for helping me get to a place where I could start writing about the new heavens and new Earth.

The two trailblazers, professors Mary Evelyn Tucker and John Grim, thank you for all your work in the Yale Forum on Religion and Ecology. I'm grateful for the ways you reach out to the Christian community in friendship to work toward restoring this sacred planet. Also, thanks goes out to the passionate folks at A Rocha USA and the Evangelical Environmental Network for your support and championing of this book.

An unlimited amount of appreciation is due to my editors,

Danielle and Bonnie. Danielle, for your shared vision and passion for this book and your encouragement and the needed reminder that it's not my magnum opus! Bonnie, you brilliantly organized and saw this project through at levels I'm not even aware of. I'm very grateful for your emphasis on the importance of the practical tips! And to the illustrator and art team—MUTI and Tiffany— thank you for bringing to life the habitats and ideas in this book in an artistic way that gives credit to the original Artist: God!

To my Creator God, who held me up under the weight of all I researched and the daily deep dives into the pain of the earth and the resulting suffering of the poor, may this book do whatever amount of good You intend for it, to heal Your Creation and lift up those harmed by environmental degradation. I'm (literally) eternally grateful for your plans for cosmic-level restoration through Christ.

Last but not least, my cat Aristotle—a true companion during the many days and nights writing tucked away during the COVID pandemic. You deserve all the salmon treats on the planet. Sustainably sourced salmon, of course.

ABOUT THE AUTHORS

Betsy Painter is an author and conservation biologist, who is passionate about environmental care and its faith-based dimensions. She has studied religion and ecology in graduate school at Yale University with a focus on the beautification of nature in the redemptive biblical narrative and its implications for environmental hope today. On the ecology side, Betsy's research interests include wetlands ecology, and she enjoys salt marsh escapades and plankton microscopy. She lives in New Haven, Connecticut, and attends St. John's Anglican/Episcopal Church. She frequents Catholic and Orthodox churches with a passion for ecumenical dialogue about creation care and its role in fostering unity within the global church.

Mark Purcell is the executive director for A Rocha USA. He began serving on its board in 2008 and joined the staff in 2016. He has a background in higher education administration and received a doctorate of education from Seattle Pacific University. Mark also worked in the Seattle technology sector for many years. He is an avid birder and lives in Austin, Texas, with his wife, Emily, where they attend Christ Church Anglican.